# PERFECTING PALEO

personalize your diet rules:
ancient wisdom meets self-testing

## ASHLEY TUDOR

Victory Belt Publishing Inc.

Las Vegas

First Published in 2014 by Victory Belt Publishing Inc.

ISBN 13: 978-1-936608-26-3

The information included in this book is for entertainment purposes only. It is not intended or implied to be
a substitute for professional medical advice. The reader
should always consult his or her healthcare provider
to determine the appropriateness of the information for
his or her own situation or with any questions regard-
ing a medical condition or treatment plan. Reading the
information in this book does not create a physician-
patient relationship.

Victory Belt® is a registered trademark of Victory Belt
Publishing Inc.
Printed in the USA
RRD 0114

To
**MOM and DAD**

# CONTENTS

# ACKNOWLEDGMENTS

*Dr. Dick Thom*, you are the Sherlock Holmes of health. You are willing to jump down the rabbit hole and explore all the issues and possibilities until they are resolved. With your clinical guidance, my passion for self-monitoring and experimentation can now be helpful to others. Your dedicated work with patients and twenty years of clinical experience lend this book credibility. Thank you for countless calls and your graceful and patient way of coaching.

*Badier Velji*, you have the remarkable talent of understanding complexity and communicating simply. Thanks for patiently teaching me, pointing me to interesting studies, and painstakingly reading over the science again and again. The world needs more passionate thinkers like you who can toggle between cutting-edge theory and practical application.

*Kelsey Marksteiner*, thank you for sharing your hard-earned scientific knowledge. I am so happy to have you as a part of my health team, and I hope we get to collaborate on future projects to help change the world. I am lucky to have you, and so are your patients!

*Gary Wolf and Kevin Kelly*, the first time I attended a Quantified Self meeting, I felt as if I had come home. The forum brought together a group of eccentric people at the edge of technology who, like me, enjoyed digging deep to uncover insight. Exposure to the tools, minds, and visualizations pushed my thinking. I eagerly awaited your monthly meetings—always insightful, surprising, and loaded with brain candy. The experimentation and self-monitoring sections of this book were inspired by you.

*Karen Boyd*, thank you for your invaluable help with the logic and flow of the copy. Your friendship is truly valued.

*Dr. Jeoff Dropbott and Dr. Lucas Tafur*, your thoughts, comments, and critiques have been invaluable.

*The staff of the Presidio branch of the San Francisco Public Library*, which has been around since long before Internet searches, I am indebted to you for your help sleuthing out resources. Full of natural light and comfortable chairs, your domain made countless hours of reading and research melt into effortless productivity. Our libraries and their staffs are a treasure.

*Finally, Mom*, you have been my supporter, my cheerleader, my proofreader, and, through it all, my friend. Without you this book would be one run-on sentence devoid of commas. Because of you this book has become more than I could have ever imagined. Thank you for patience and commitment that mirrored my own.

# INTRODUCTION

The Paleo diet is simple. Eat food—meats, vegetables, nuts, seeds, some starch, some fruit, no sugar. These simple guidelines allow food to be a powerful tool in the arsenal of health. No more counting calories, no more weighing and measuring. Paleo guides us to eat what nature has provided and what our bodies were designed to eat.

Individual by individual, news of the Paleo diet's merits is spreading to the mainstream. People are losing weight, coming out of their diet-induced mental fogs, and regaining energy in body and mind. Beyond making us more attractive, the Paleo diet is reversing diseases such as diabetes, heart disease, and autoimmune conditions. Food is once again becoming the foundation of good health.

Why, then, do some people thrive on the Paleo diet while others struggle? Despite the simplicity of the Paleo diet, it is clear that there is no one-size-fits-all rule book. Diet—and, more broadly, health—is personal. While one template works for some, it falls short for others.

This book offers a conceptual framework to help you uncover the diet rules that work for you. It simplifies the complex ecology of the body into four easy-to-understand integrated systems—food, hormones, inflammation, and activity. With a basic understanding of how these systems work together, you can utilize self-monitoring tools to track, test, and optimize your standings in each category, starting with the goals that are most important to you. With a clear framework and the aid of technology, you can learn to speak the language of your unique body and come to your own conclusions. Your body, your rules. With an ancient diet and modern tools, you can be healthier than ever before. And that is powerful stuff.

# PART I

## SMART FOODS

Nutritional starvation in
the era of supermarkets

## Chapter 1

# DESIGNED FOR A DIFFERENT WORLD

## Food technologies have changed; our bodies have not

## THE WAY WE WERE
## VERSUS THE WAY WE ARE NOW

Human DNA, the body's manual for interpreting everything it encounters, evolved millions of years ago in a world drastically different from our own. Our primal ancestors worked hard for the foods they ate. With only basic tools and fire, they hunted animals, collected and prepared wild vegetables, and destroyed deadly microbes by cooking and preserving their meals. Over time, evolution designed their bodies to thrive on the foods that were available in their environment.

Survival required energy-rich fat to fuel activity, seasonal sugar to add extra fat stores for winter, and the occasional mineral salt to balance fluids in the body. But the varying availability of foods meant that these necessities were not always around. When they were available, our ancestors had to take advantage and eat up. Gorging in a time of plenty was valuable genetic programming that would save them in a later time of scarcity.

Some 10,000 years ago—not long ago in terms of human evolution—the world changed. Farming was introduced. It revolutionized human communities, lifestyles, and diets. Food sources became more consistent. Since cultivating and harvesting crops required people to remain in one place for longer periods, populations settled and swelled. But the farmed crops differed from the foods that our ancestors had gathered. We lost the diversity that our hunter-gatherer ancestors had enjoyed and the nutritional richness that variety had brought. This transition came at a cost to human health and quality of life. Insufficient time to adapt to the new diet and a lack of evolutionary pressure put hunter-gatherers' DNA at odds with the new world unfolding around them.

As farming developed and trade expanded, the foundation of the human diet shifted to simple carbohydrates in the forms of sugar, molasses, white flour, and white rice. A funny thing began to happen: the human body changed. People shrank in size. Teeth began to decay and grow crooked. People started to experience the "diseases of civilization," such as heart disease, obesity, hypertension, type 2 diabetes, autoimmune disease, and osteoporosis. Meanwhile, isolated populations that continued to live as their ancestors had remained tall and strong, with straight teeth and few incidents of cancer or degenerative diseases.

More recently, new technologies were developed to tinker with foods, causing new side effects. Oils, sugars, and refined cereals were engineered to satisfy our genetic preferences for these foods—preferences that had been set in a different world, one in which essential fats, sugars, and salt were scarce. Our bodies were programmed to find fats, sugars, and salt irresistible so that when they were available, we would gorge on them. With new food technologies designed to increase shelf life (extreme heating, irradiation, ionization, and pasteurization), these foods became ever present, yet we still gorge.

Farming and food technologies have resulted in supermarket shelves brimming with seemingly endless food choices. But while the choices seem vast, we have actually lost diversity in our diet. Where we once enjoyed foods that varied according to season, geography, and climate, today the types of foods we eat have narrowed. Most packaged foods are made from wheat and corn. But the lack of diversity does not stop there. Many of the fruits and vegetables we get from supermarkets are of plant strains that stand up to shipping around the world and look good on the produce stand. Abundance of food choice has translated into not more food diversity but less.

## THE WESTERN DIET'S EFFECT ON ISOLATED POPULATIONS

With the advent of colonialism and the adoption of the Western diet around the globe, scientists, doctors, and dentists set out to study populations that had not been exposed to a diet of grains and refined sugar. They found that these populations, across all variations in geography, climate, or natural food sources, had bright smiles with straight teeth. While some suffered from contagious diseases due to poor sanitation, most were strong, healthy, and free of cancer and degenerative diseases. As wheat, sugar, and molasses were introduced, these populations changed for the worse within a short period.

No one can tell the stories of these isolated people better than the diligent researchers who studied and recorded the changes within these populations as the Western diet was introduced. Such individuals include George Catlin among the Plains Indians; John Rae, Frederick Schwatka, and Vilhjalmur

Stefansson among the Inuit; John Orr and J. L. Gilkes among the Masai; and Staffan Lindeberg among the Kitavans. Their firsthand accounts make for fascinating reading. If you are interested in learning more, here are some good books to check out:

*Nutrition and Physical Degeneration* by Weston A. Price

*Food and Western Disease: Health and Nutrition from an Evolutionary Perspective* by Staffan Lindeberg

*Physiological and Medical Observations Among the Indians of Southwestern United States and Northern Mexico* by Ales Hrdlicka

# MODERN FOOD TECHNOLOGY—
# NOT AS GOOD AS NATURE'S COMPLEXITY

Take a bite of a ripe, juicy heirloom tomato. Flavors dance in your mouth as the juiciness explodes. Compare this experience to eating a store-bought tomato. A bite does not melt; it crunches or, worse, dissolves into mealy blandness. Flavors fall flat. Tomatoes and other seasonal produce are now available year-round thanks to farmers and food scientists. While they appeal to our eyes in the market, our taste buds don't rejoice in their diminished flavor.

Today, decisions about what to grow are based on maximizing yield and shelf life and making shipping and storing as easy as possible. What is produced and sold is what is commercially viable. What is commercially viable is not always the healthiest or best tasting. Commercial farmers replace compost, nature's fertilizer, with synthetic fertilizers full of nitrogen, potassium, and phosphorus because they produce high yields. But plants need much more to thrive. In this case, quantity replaces quality. Despite greater yields, the soil is depleted, and our foods don't contain the complexity of nutrients that they once gained from nature's richness. Just take the difference between a store-bought tomato and the real thing. Taste—and nutrients—are lost when we tinker with nature's complexity.

The same can be said for the way we treat our foods in order to extend shelf life. Nutrients are actually removed from many foods to allow them to keep longer. For example, flour used to be a perishable food. Then somebody figured out that the nutrients ("germ") that critters like to eat could be removed, making flour last longer. This technology made flour a commercially viable product, but at the expense of the nutrients it originally contained. And what is done with the nutrients stripped from the wheat used to make flour? They are added to smoothies or other "nutritional" supplements!

All this technology was created to make food grow all the time, regardless of season, and last longer. It doesn't mean that we have a solid understanding of food science. We supposedly know more about food than ever before—but where has all this understanding of science and food technology gotten us?

## FRANKENFOODS AND TECHNOLOGY GONE AWRY

Technological food innovations can be beneficial or harmful. Using fire to kill microbes is good. Irradiating foods to increase shelf stabilization is bad, as it destroys nutrients along with microbes. Drying and curing meats to sustain their longevity is good. Refining vegetable oils so that they can sit on the shelf for years is bad. Meat with a side of vegetables is good. An energy bar to replace a meal is bad. Good technology helps us prepare and cook foods, adds to the diversity of the foods we eat, and helps us carry healthy food on the go. Modern processing methods strip nutrients from foods and leave us with food imposters that degrade our health.

In the last few decades, we have been given frankenfoods—monster-like creations stitched together using various modern technologies in an attempt to create the ideal commercially viable foods. Zap for shelf stabilization. Spray with vitamins for better nutritional labeling. Enhance taste with artificial flavors. Alter textures with additives. Entomb in plastic to lengthen shelf life. The result: a monster, the frankenfood.

Today these frankenfoods crowd supermarket shelves and make up the bulk of the Western world's diet. But these are not the foods that best serve our well-being. If we want to optimize health and performance, we need to eat as we were programmed to eat.

# GOOD FOOD-PROCESSING TECHNOLOGIES

## Cooking
Preparing food by the process of heat. Kills or deactivates potential harmful organisms, such as bacteria and viruses. Destroys antinutrients in some plants and improves digestibility.

## Drying
Removing water from food via evaporation (air-drying, sun-drying, or wind-drying) for the purpose of preservation.

## Smoking
Adding flavor to, cooking, or preserving foods by exposing them to burning or smoldering plant material.

## Salting
Preserving foods by adding edible salt. Kills most bacterial fungi and other pathogenic organisms.

## Fermenting
Anaerobically breaking down energy-rich compounds, such as carbohydrates, using yeasts and bacteria in a controlled manner.

## Storing
Setting aside for later use in dry, cool spaces, including cellars and mounds.

# BAD FOOD-PROCESSING TECHNOLOGIES

## Irradiation

Process by which a food is exposed to radiation in order to sterilize it. Irradiation not only strips food of bacteria and viruses but also zaps nutrients.

## Pasteurization

Process of heating foods to a certain temperature for a specified period. Pasteurization is used to slow microbial growth to extend shelf life. It destroys enzymes and beneficial microbes.

## Additives

Substances added to foods to enhance flavor, appearance, and/or shelf life. Food additives include anticaking agents, antifoaming agents, antioxidants, bulk agents, food coloring, color retention agents, emulsifiers, flavor enhancers, glazing agents, preservatives, stabilizers, sweeteners, and thickeners.

## Fortification

Process of adding micronutrients to foods. Food producers add or spray nutrients that are thought to be healthy and are destroyed in the stabilization process.

## Plastic Packaging

Material used to enclose or protect products for storage, large-scale distribution, and sale. When foods are brought to high temperatures, as in a microwave, plasticizers in the plastics can leach into the foods, especially if the foods are high in fat.

# THE PALEO DIET: A TOOL TO HELP
# IDENTIFY THE FOODS THAT OUR BODIES
# WERE MEANT TO CONSUME

As bad food technologies continue to sneak into the most innocent food sources, many people have decided to turn to the foods of our ancestors of the Paleolithic period, the earliest period of the Stone Age, in order to avoid the unhealthy choices that pervade the modern food industry. A Paleo diet focuses on the foods that our bodies are most likely to thrive on after hundreds of thousands of years of evolution. They are the foods that our hunter-gatherer ancestors ate: wild animals, fish, vegetables, and seasonal fruit.

A Paleo diet tries to closely mimic the diet of our ancestors using these guidelines: meats, vegetables, nuts, seeds, some starch, little fruit, and no sugar. This regimen has helped thousands of people regain control of their health and bodies and reverse chronic diseases. Devoid of grains, refined sugars, legumes, and dairy, the Paleo diet is nutritionally dense on a calorie-for-calorie basis. The following books are worth a read for a detailed discussion of the diet:

*The Paleo Solution: The Original Human Diet* by Robb Wolf

*The Primal Blueprint: Reprogram Your Genes for Effortless Weight Loss, Vibrant Health, and Boundless Energy* by Mark Sisson

*The Paleo Diet: Lose Weight and Get Healthy by Eating the Foods You Were Designed to Eat* by Loren Cordain

# PART II

## STOP SURVIVING, START THRIVING

A new equation for optimal health

## Chapter 2

# FOOD: NOT ALL CALORIES ARE CREATED EQUAL

Why fats won't make you fat, bad carbs are health culprits, and fructose gives you the liver of an alcoholic

## FROM TRAINS TO GRAINS:
## THE DUBIOUS ORIGINS OF THE CALORIE

Ask dieters what the key to weight loss is and they will tell you it's to burn more calories than you eat. This idea has become so deified in the minds of many that it is now the single most popular tool used for dieting. A product's calorie count has become so important that it has even migrated to the front label on some packaged goods. Even indulgent foods like cookies, juice, and alcohol boast low-calorie versions. *Low-calorie* has become synonymous with *healthy*. Where did this ubiquitous unit of measure come from, and how much does it actually tell us?

The calorie is a measurement that was invented during the Industrial Revolution. It was conceived in the early nineteenth century by French physicist and chemist Nicolas Clément, who, among many other pursuits, studied the thermodynamics of steam in relation to powering steam engines. He came up with the notion of the calorie to provide a metric to accurately describe the potential energy of fuel. Clément defined 1 calorie as the quantity of energy needed to raise the temperature of 1 kilogram of water by 1 degree Celsius.

A few decades later, a nutritionist named Wilbur Olin Atwater was seeking to understand the potential energy in food. His thought was that bodies are machines and food is the fuel that runs those machines, and that meant he could apply Clément's notion of potential energy to food. Instead of incinerating coal or wood, he incinerated foods such as mutton, rye bread, and pickled herring in a device called a *calorimeter*. Different foods produced varying levels of heat. He reasoned that each food had a different energy potential; some burned fast and hot while others burned slow and steady. With this information, Atwater created a table of the caloric values of popular foods. The notion of calories caught on.

A calorie is an appealing metric unit. It represents the potential energy in a food—a simple concept to grasp. This simplicity explains why calories have become the focal point of conversations about diet and nutrition. If our bellies were incinerators and powered our bodies through combustion, calories would be a useful metric. However, our bodies are more complex than steam engines. There's more to food than the energy it gives off. A calorie, which is determined just by how fast and hot a food burns, is too simplistic a metric on which to base our understanding of nutrition.

> If our bellies were incinerators and powered our bodies through combustion, calories would be a useful metric.

The calorie does not measure or make any distinction in the way the body processes different kinds of foods. If we want to move the conversation beyond oversimplified nutritional concepts, we have to understand more about

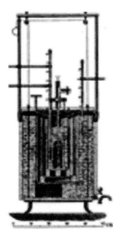

**The calorimeter used for Atwater's experiments**

Inside this device is a small cylinder in which the substance to be tested is burned. The small cylinder is encased within a larger cylinder that holds water. The heat from the burning substance is transferred to the water and measured by the rise in the water's temperature, as shown by a thermometer.

how the body works—how it breaks down food and what happens afterward. When armed with more knowledge, we can better understand what our bodies ask of us and respond appropriately.

## OPTIMAL HEALTH IS MORE THAN COUNTING CALORIES

The calorie argument claims that, based on weight, age, and other variables, each person needs a specific number of calories per day. To lose, gain, or maintain weight in this model, two variables are in play: calories consumed and calories expended.

According to this theory, to lose weight we simply eat less and move more. To gain weight, we move less and eat more. If we followed this simplified formula, we could eat Twinkies all day and run those calories off on a treadmill. However, common sense tells us that this is not healthy. Sure, counting calories can help some people move in the right direction by eliminating the most egregious diet offenders, but for those who are serious about being healthy, simply counting calories doesn't make the cut. Counting calories does not help manage appetite or eliminate cravings, and these factors can be serious impediments to weight loss. It also doesn't help manage or reverse diseases. We need a more holistic model.

Weight loss is one of the biggest single motivators for making dietary changes, but optimizing our health offers a full slate of additional benefits. When we are thriving, we are lean, strong, and full of energy. We are emotionally steady. We even have clearer skin. As a considerable added bonus, seeking optimal health today has a big payoff as we grow older.

## THE FOUR PILLARS OF HEALTH: FOOD, HORMONES, INFLAMMATION, AND ACTIVITY

When we start looking closely at the body, the science can get complicated fast. The good news is, we need to know only the basic concepts of each pillar of health in order to reap most of the benefits.

When thinking about the **food** pillar, you need to know how your body deals with the major macronutrients, specifically carbohydrates. For **hormones**, you need to understand how your diet affects fat storage through the hormone insulin and the stress hormone cortisol. For **inflammation**, you need to understand how the foods you eat affect chronic inflammation. Finally, you need to look at your physical **activity** and see how it can be maximized to bolster your health.

These pillars form the foundation of optimal health. Because they work in combination, the concept of the four pillars is a bit more sophisticated than a simple calculation of calories in, calories out. While food choice plays the largest role, you also need to think about how the foods you choose affect your hormones, inflammation, and ability to participate in physical activities. Making the right changes in what you eat will positively affect every system in your body.

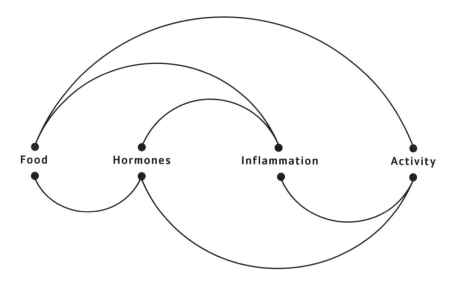

## Food ↔ Activity

Eating the right foods makes you energetic and compels you to be active. Eating the wrong foods leaves you feeling lethargic and depleted.

## Food ↔ Hormones

Eating large amounts of carbohydrates triggers the release of a hormone called insulin. One of insulin's roles is to send a signal to cells that they should absorb glucose from the bloodstream. When carbohydrates are broken down into sugar (glucose), insulin helps shuttle excess glucose out of the bloodstream and into the cells. Muscles and the liver fill up first. When they run out of room and blood glucose is still high, insulin shuttles that extra energy to be stored as fat.

## Food ↔ Inflammation

Eating the wrong foods wreaks havoc on the gut, weakening its defense against bad particles (undigested food, bacteria, and other alien substances) that want to get into the bloodstream. When the invaders make it into the blood, the body fights back with an immune response, which triggers inflammation.

## Inflammation ↔ Hormones

Inflammation makes the body more resistant to the hormone insulin. When the body becomes insulin-resistant, this hormone becomes less effective at doing its job. This means more insulin is needed to do the same amount of work. The pancreas (the body's insulin factory) tires out.

## Activity ↔ Hormones

Activity elicits the right hormonal cocktail, stimulating the body to rebuild and strengthen itself. Overtraining, however, puts excessive stress on the endocrine system (hormone factories). It gets run-down and overworked and is unable to do its job effectively (adrenal fatigue).

## Activity ↔ Inflammation

Strenuous activity breaks down muscle tissue, causing inflammation. When athletes engage in constant rigorous exercise, they can suffer from invisible chronic inflammation inside the body and in the bloodstream.

# HOW THE BODY TURNS FOOD INTO FUEL:
# THE DISASSEMBLY LINE OF DIGESTION

Food supplies the raw material for the body's basic functions, growth and repair. When you eat, your body begins to disassemble food into usable nutrients, including the three macronutrients: carbohydrates, proteins, and fats. These nutrients play different but essential roles.

## CARBOHYDRATES

Carbohydrates serve as fast-acting fuel for your cells. When they enter your system, they are broken down into simple sugars, including glucose, lactose, and fructose. The body utilizes these sugars differently: glucose is sent directly into the bloodstream to feed the activity, repair, and replication of cells; lactose is digested into even smaller sugars, galactose and glucose; and fructose is sent to the liver to be processed and stored.

Glucose is the most common of these simple sugars. It fuels your muscles and metabolism. Most important, glucose fuels the brain. The brain needs more glucose than other organs, requiring a steady stream to keep up with its list of functions.

Carbohydrates and the sugars into which they are broken down are processed at varying speeds. Complex carbohydrates, which include vegetables such as broccoli, kale, and sweet potatoes, are full of fiber, so they take longer to break down. Complex carbohydrates slow the rate at which foods move through the stomach (gastric emptying) and determine the speed of nutrient absorption. Simple carbohydrates, such as sugar and candy, enter the bloodstream quickly, providing a jolt of energy in the form of a glucose surge. Fruit and packaged foods contain a significant amount of fructose, a simple sugar that goes straight to the liver (where much of it is turned into fat) instead of to hungry cells. Later in this chapter we will explore the different journeys of glucose and fructose and the consequences those journeys have on our health.

Glucose is the energy that powers your cells. At times you have more glucose circulating in your system than is needed for immediate use. The body prudently wants to store glucose for later and sends it to one of three storage banks.

The muscles act as the first storage bank, storing glucose to fuel bursts of intense activity. This energy is easy to access. Since muscles lack the enzyme that exports glucose from cells, the glucose in muscles is destined to fuel activity. While storing glucose in muscle cells is desirable, storage space is limited.

Excess glucose is sent to the liver for storage. The liver is a flexible energy bank that deals with deposits (excess glucose in the system) and withdrawals (glucose sent into the system when glucose is low). Energy stored in the liver is easy to access and steadies the body's glucose levels between meals and during sleep. Like muscles, the liver has a finite storage capacity. When it is full, excess energy is sent into long-term storage.

Fat, or adipose tissue, is the body's third storage bank and is reserved for long-term deposits. You are born with a given number of fat cells, which expand and contract based on how much extra energy they are storing. When the body has enough energy in the muscles and liver, the excess makes its way into long-term storage: the fat cells. This fat is kept as insurance against scarcity in the future and is harder for the body to access than the energy stored

> **Fat is the body's storage bank. The body does not easily give up these stores.**

in the muscles and liver. The body does not easily give up these stores. It takes the trouble to release this energy only when glucose levels in the rest of the body are low or during extended moderate exercise.

Carbs are not the only source of glucose. The body can also derive glucose from fats and proteins. However, since the process of turning these other macronutrients into glucose takes more time, your body directs you to eat carbs when you crave energy. Like an addict who knows how to get a quick fix, your body knows what will get glucose into the bloodstream fastest: carbs! Like other substances that provide an immediate boost, they are addictive.

## PROTEIN

Protein, whose name is derived from the Greek word for "of prime importance," is the body's fundamental building material. Protein is required for the operation of every cell's metabolic activity. It is the second most common molecule in the body, after water. The brain, bones, skin, muscles, blood, hair, and connective tissue are all made up primarily of protein. Protein also forms the antibodies that the body creates to fight off disease, as well as some hormones that regulate activity.

When you eat protein, your body breaks it down into its basic building blocks—amino acids. These amino acids can then be reassembled into the various proteins necessary for the body's essential activities, such as the construction of bones, muscles, cartilage, skin, and blood. Amino acids are also used to make enzymes and hormones. As soon as protein enters the digestive system, it begins to be broken down and put to work. Unlike carbohydrates or fats, protein is not stored. However, if there is more protein then can be immediately used by the body, excess protein is turned into glucose.

Twenty different amino acids are incorporated into various peptides (two or more amino acids coupled by a peptide bond) and proteins. Your body can manufacture some of them, but nine of those amino acids come only from food: plants, poultry, meat, fish, nuts, and eggs.

When you eat protein, hormones released in the stomach and gut make you feel satiated. These "enough-to-eat" hormones (cholecystokinin, peptide YY, ghrelin, and insulin) signal the body to stop eating.

When carbohydrate intake is limited and blood glucose is low, the body utilizes glucogenic amino acids (found in protein) to make glucose. The process, called *gluconeogenesis*, is slow but provides a stable, though limited, source of glucose.

## FATS

Fats are essential to the human body. They are broken down into fatty acids that help form cell membranes and hormones. They are also stored throughout the body and are available for use as an energy source or to regulate body temperature and cushion the organs.

In times of need, the liver can convert fats into glucose, the body's go-go juice. For the body to make one glucose molecule, two triglyceride (fat) molecules are required. The process is inefficient and demands extra resources. As a result, the body will not go to the trouble of dipping into fat stores unless dietary sugars are low.

> The body will not go to the trouble of dipping into fat stores unless glucose in the diet is low.

Like protein, fats trigger the release of "I'm full" hormones. Because fats take a long time to break down in the digestive system, the feeling of fullness lasts longer.

In general, when you consume more calories from fat and protein than from carbs, your body begins the transition to burning its own fat—the excess fat on your tush and belly. It takes some time for your body to adjust to processing this new form of fuel, but once your primary source of fuel has shifted from carbs to fat, you are said to be "fat-adapted." That's a good thing!

When carbs are severely limited in your diet, you enter into ketosis, a state of intense fat burning. The ketogenic diet is getting more and more attention, as doctors have been using it to battle cancer, eliminate epileptic seizures, and prevent the progression of degenerative brain diseases such as Alzheimer's. To learn more about ketosis, see page 156.

## TIPS FOR MANAGING YOUR CRAVINGS

Your body asks, sometimes shouts, for what it needs. These cravings can be so strong that they are impossible to ignore. The trick is to manage these messages so that they don't derail your diet. Resisting food is not about willpower—it's about interpreting the body's message correctly. To do so, you need to understand the reason behind your body's request.

**Be sure you are hungry.** Before eating, take a moment to listen to your body. Are you eating because you are bored? Do you need a break? Are you perpetuating a bad habit? If the answer to any of these questions is yes, change your space. Go for a walk or sit in a different spot. This change in physical environment can shift your mind and provide the extra stimulation needed to shrug off a bad habit. If you feel you are genuinely hungry, eat smartly.

**Drink a glass of water before you eat.** What we think is hunger is often thirst that's misinterpreted. Before sitting down to an unscheduled meal or snack, drink a glass of water. Wait half an hour and then check in with your body again.

**Eat the foods your body needs, not what it asks for.** If your blood sugar is low, your body will often ask for the foods that provide the quickest energy: sweets or other fast-acting fuels. Eat protein or fat to meet your body's short-term needs and even-out long-term energy. A handful of nuts, a spoonful of almond butter, a piece of chicken, or a couple of slices of deli meat will serve you better and get you off the energy roller coaster. Properly fed, your body will stop craving sugar. Willpower no longer has to be the factor that determines your success.

**Don't drink sugar water.** When your body asks for soda or juice, it's saying, "I'm thirsty"—but it is also saying, "Why drink water when I can have extra sugar to store up fat for the coming winter?" Unless you want to store lots of excess fat in your cells, choose water over juice. You can find your vitamins in healthier places.

**Eat before you are desperate.** Desperation is a powerful force to derail your diet. Don't get stuck without good fuel. Store stashes of fats and protein—such as beef jerky, tuna packs, and single-serving nut butter packets—in your desk, glove box, or bag.

# WHY SOME FOODS
# LEAVE YOU FEELING FATIGUED

As you eat, nutrients are not digested in the order in which they enter your body. Instead, they are prioritized according to how fast the body can break them down. Carbohydrates, the fastest to process into simple-sugar fuel, are absorbed first. Proteins, which are broken down into component amino acids, are next. Finally, the body tackles fats.

Foods that burn slowly, such as fats and proteins, provide a consistent stream of energy, making you feel full and satisfied longer. Carbohydrates, on the other hand, are processed comparatively quickly, giving you spikes of sugar in the bloodstream.

Simple carbs create a KABAM! in your system. Sugars give the initial feelings of superhuman energy, giddiness, and invincibility, like a junkie on crack. However, this high soon comes crashing down, often resulting in low energy or motivation and the need for a nap. The nutritionally unaware eat their way out of this inevitable slump by ingesting more carbs, spiking blood sugar back up and continuing the yo-yo effect throughout the day. Little do they know that turning to this so-called solution only intensifies the problem.

In the 1800s, when many sawmills were buzzing, big logs were cut into planks for building. The process of cutting those logs resulted in various sizes of wood scraps, from large chunks to sawdust. Some of the wood dust was so fine that the particles floated into the air, filling the sawmill. With this volatile, combustible air in a confined space, smoking at a sawmill was dangerous. Sometimes sparks or other flames caught the air on fire, causing huge explosions.

Carbohydrates are like the different sizes of wood in the sawmill. Do you want to know what soda and juice do to your system? These simple carbohydrates are like the wood dust in the air that can combust, exploding in your system and wreaking havoc. Complex carbohydrates are much less dangerous. They are like the larger chunks of wood, which may take some time to get started but provide excellent fuel and burn in a controlled way. The fiber in complex-carb foods like broccoli, kale, and cauliflower slows the glucose dump into your system. A steady stream of glucose rather than a quick flood enables your body to manage energy flows more efficiently and without the energy crash later. Properly fueled in this way, you can run circles around your friends and colleagues all afternoon while they sit in their post-lunch haze.

## THE CARBOHYDRATE SPECTRUM

Simple carbs enter the system quickly. Complex carbs take longer. Proteins and fat are absorbed the slowest. Given the same number of calories, the illustration below gives you an idea of the rates at which various types of carbohydrates enter the body.

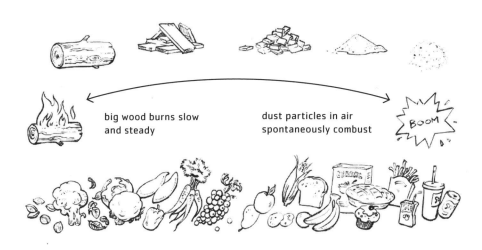

big wood burns slow and steady

dust particles in air spontaneously combust

BOOM

## IDEAL GLUCOSE CHART

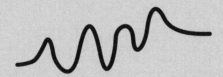

- Steady glucose release means consistent energy throughout the day.

- Body feels alert and sharp and has optimal energy without receiving cues to store more fat.

- Absence of dips in glucose keeps ravenous hunger at bay.

## NON-IDEAL GLUCOSE CHART

- Big swings in energy are experienced, with pronounced highs followed by lows shortly after eating meals.

- Low-glucose periods are characterized by lack of energy, sleepiness, mental fogginess, and hunger, even after eating.

- Low levels of glucose trigger the body to be hungry more often.

- Coping mechanisms are developed to deal with lows, including eating, caffeinating, sleeping, or even exercising.

- Spikes in glucose are hard for the body to manage. As stress piles upon stress, "glucose creep" develops, and glucose levels rise throughout the day.

- Consistently high blood sugar can lead to chronically elevated insulin. The result? Your body never dips into fat stores, and you pile on weight without being able to burn it off. Combined with leptin resistance (due to elevated triglycerides—see page 62), high inflammation, and intestinal permeability (see page 71), you have a recipe for obesity and autoimmune diseases.

## CARB MONSTERS AND THE DANGER OF OVER-SUGARING YOUR KIDS

Kids are cute, except when they are not. Often bad parenting is not to blame. The culprit is bad feeding. Pint-sized people experience extreme swings of blood sugar on diets high in carb-rich foods—such as fruit juice, cereals, and bagels—which cause momentary bursts of energy followed by crashes. If you were on a sugar-induced roller coaster, you would be yelling, screaming, and stomping your feet in public as well. Excessive sugar consumption influences everything, including mood, attention span, energy, and cognitive ability. For kids, this translates to tantrums, hyperactivity, attention deficit hyperactivity disorder, and poor performance in school.

Just like adults, kids need quality food. Even if they are less self-aware, their little bodies and brains react to the octane in their systems. Set them up for success. Give them real nutrition.

## TIPS FOR TEACHING
## KIDS GOOD EATING BEHAVIORS

**Say no to juice.** Feeding your child juice is like serving up a liquefied candy bar. If you must serve juice, dilute it generously with water. If flavor is what your kids are after, check out non-juice options, such as Hint water, which infuses fruits without adding sugar or scary preservatives. Kids lived without juice for thousands of years. They can live without it now.

**If food is entertainment, choose your treats wisely.** If keeping your babes occupied and quiet is the goal, try giving them goodies that won't spike their blood sugar. Make your own treats ahead of time and dole them out when you are ready for a little peace and quiet.

**Make snack time health food time.** Grab-and-go, prepackaged convenience foods fill kids up with empty calories, make them overexcited, and leave them in a sugar-induced daze. Instead, serve vegetables when kids are hungry on the playground and in the sandbox. Kids will learn to love what you give them. The sooner you get them going on nature's finest, the more they will love, crave, and ask for it.

**Energy bars are not for small people.** Don't be a sucker for marketing. Energy bars are just socially permissible candy bars. If you want to feed your kid candy, own up to it and feed them candy. Just because energy bars claim to be good for athletes doesn't mean that they are good for kids.

**Model good behavior.** Monkey see, monkey do. Your kids will love what you love. Fill your plate with good foods, and they will learn to do the same. Unfortunately, lots of kids pick up unhealthy cues from television commercials and schoolmates. Be vigilant about setting a good example.

**Prepare foods with your kids.** We all love what we make. It's no different for kids. Help them play a part in food preparation and cooking. Chances are they will be more invested in eating their own nutritious concoctions.

**Stay away from the kids' menu.** Forty years ago, kids' menus did not exist. Avoid at all costs the kaleidoscope of processed browns and tans: chicken nuggets, hot dogs, mac and cheese, fries, and so on. Feed your kids the same kinds of foods that you would eat. Smaller portions are good, but different foods are not. Color can be a helpful guide—fill your child's plate with the full range of colors found in nature's foods.

**Pack your kids' lunches.** No one is more invested in your family's health than you. School lunches are determined by prices and politics, and bad carbs win both battles. Keep your kids thriving by packing good, nutritious foods. Their better grades and teachers' good reports will make the extra effort worth it. Bad nutrition can result in misbehavior, attention deficit hyperactivity disorder, and a reliance on prescription medications for problems that could have been avoided with good food.

**Don't reward with food.** Our happy places are set early in life. When we grow up and life gets tough, we turn to those patterned behaviors for comfort in bad times. Set the foundation for a good relationship with food from an early age by giving your children non-food rewards.

**Supervise sport snacks.** Drinks and snacks that are marketed to athletes are high in carbs and sugar. They should not be on Little League refreshment tables. Just because your kids are running around on a playing field does not mean that you should let them drink or eat sugar. Instead, find alternative beverages and snacks to keep your children fueled with the good stuff.

# MANAGING CARBOHYDRATES: GET ENERGY THROUGH NATURE'S FOODS

Carbs are typically the foundation of every meal in the Standard American Diet, but they are overrated compared to their macronutrient companions, protein and fat. While protein and fat provide sustained energy, carbs in their common processed form just give you a boom-and-bust. Get off the roller coaster. Replace fast (simple) carbs from sugars and grains with slow (complex) carbs from nature's vegetable bounty.

## WHAT YOU CAN DO ABOUT CARBS FOR OPTIMAL HEALTH

**Replace fast-burning foods**, such as wheat-based products (bread, pasta, and cereal), with slow-burning foods, such as vegetables and proteins.

**Manage your cravings smartly** by eating foods that fuel your body (fat, protein, and slow-burning carbs), not by giving in to what it asks for (sweets, sugar, and bad, simple carbs).

# THE ROLE OF SUGAR IN EVOLUTIONARY BIOLOGY

When humans were hunter-gatherers long ago, the seasons played a big role. How we adapted to the availability of food during times of plenty affected survival when the pickings were scarce. We evolved in a time when food was not abundant, and the body developed clever strategies to compensate. Response to sweetness was one of them.

As summer came into full bloom and trees were heavy with fruit, nature's bounties were plentiful. For a short period, we had access to more food than we needed to meet our immediate survival needs. The body learned to take advantage of the abundance in this short season to prepare for winter. This meant taking in excess sugar from fruit and storing it as fat. To do so, we needed to eat, eat, and eat without getting full. Fructose, the sugar found in fruit, bypassed the mechanism for fullness so that we could eat until fruit was no longer available and thereby plump up for the coming scarcity.

> Fructose, the sugar found in fruit, bypassed the mechanism for fullness so that we could eat and eat to plump up for the coming scarcity of winter. The problem today is that winter never comes.

The body's strategy for dealing with this once-seasonal sugar allowed it to pack away reserves for later in the form of fat. When winter came and nourishment was scarce, the body would dip into fat storage for needed energy. The process of breaking down fat into fuel for the body results in glucose and a by-product called *ketone bodies* (a metabolic equivalent of glucose), fuel that keeps us going in times of scarcity. The problem today is that winter never comes. We no longer face those periods of scarcity that cued the dip into fat storage. We have also upped the amount of sugar in our diets. Thus we store more and more fat without ever clearing out the storage bins.

# NOT ALL SUGARS ARE CREATED EQUAL

As mentioned previously, the body breaks down carbohydrates into three types of simple sugar for processing—glucose, fructose, and galactose. Foods that are sweet to the taste have some combination of these molecules. For example, sucrose, or common table sugar, is made up of one glucose molecule and one fructose molecule. The dairy sugar lactose, on the other hand, is made up of one galactose molecule and one glucose molecule.

These three different crystalline structures common in food have different levels of sweetness. Fructose is the sweetest of all naturally occurring carbohydrates—sweeter than any other sugar. Glucose is the next sweetest, while galactose is much less sweet.

The sugars differ by more than just varying sweetness levels; their chemical makeups have important health implications as well. Glucose and fructose have different chemical structures that affect the ways the body processes and metabolizes them.

To understand their unique roles in human biology, let's follow their paths through the body. When you take a big bite of cake, it travels to the stomach, where the cake is churned and broken apart by stomach acid. Once the cake has been mashed up into smaller particles, it travels to the small intestine. When the sucrose, or table sugar, in the cake hits the intestinal wall, the molecules are broken into their two main components, glucose and fructose. Once separated, these molecules go off on their own paths.

> **Glucose can be utilized by every cell in the body. Fructose can be metabolized only by the liver, where it is likely turned into fat.**

Glucose goes directly into the bloodstream and can be utilized by every cell in the body. The cells use it to fuel the brain, to rebuild muscles, or to go about daily life.

In contrast, most fructose can be metabolized only by the liver, which has special enzymes to break it down. So instead of moving throughout the entire body, fructose must travel through the liver to be metabolized and turned into energy. As you can imagine, if you increase the amount of fructose you consume, your liver will have lots of extra work to do.

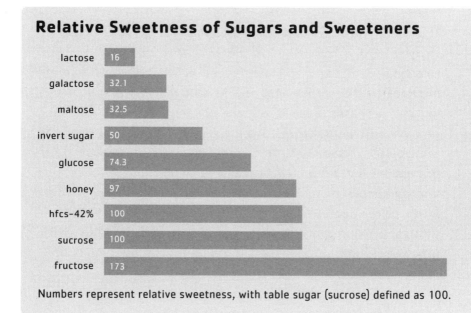

**Relative Sweetness of Sugars and Sweeteners**

| | |
|---|---|
| lactose | 16 |
| galactose | 32.1 |
| maltose | 32.5 |
| invert sugar | 50 |
| glucose | 74.3 |
| honey | 97 |
| hfcs–42% | 100 |
| sucrose | 100 |
| fructose | 173 |

Numbers represent relative sweetness, with table sugar (sucrose) defined as 100.

## FRUCTOSE: FROM RARE TREAT TO UBIQUITOUS COMMODITY

Long ago, fructose was relatively scarce in the human diet. Fruit and other fructose-filled goodies were generally available for only a short time, and people often had to compete with other sugar-loving animals to win our share of the spoils. Since this sugar was so valuable, the way the body processed this rare commodity was an asset for survival.

Today, fructose is abundant. Fruits, once available only seasonally, are now ready to eat every day of the year. And over the centuries, fruits have been selectively bred for higher sweetness levels—which means more fructose. Every day many people dress their morning breakfasts with these colorful sugar bombs and slurp liquid fructose (also known as juice), delivering a concentrated blast of fructose to the liver.

## HOW ORANGE JUICE BECAME A BREAKFAST STAPLE

Orange juice became commercialized in 1910. Overproduction of citrus fruit that year meant that crop prices were plummeting and orchards were in danger of being cut down. Seeking new ways to market their surplus, orange growers applied the technology of pasteurization to kill bacteria that cause rot in orange juice. This extra processing made juice shelf-stable and shippable to cities around the country. Because of its lower price, pasteurized orange juice replaced the more traditional breakfast accompaniment of stewed fruit, thus stripping the traditional breakfast of its beneficial fiber while adding even more fructose to the mix.

Beyond occurring naturally in fruit, fructose has made its way into just about every packaged food in the form of high-fructose corn syrup (HFCS). HFCS is a particularly insidious form of sugar that is refined from corn instead of sugarcane or beets. Technically known by the food industry as HFCS-55 (a concoction composed of 55 percent fructose and 45 percent glucose), it was created to be indistinguishable from sucrose to the palate. In addition to providing good flavor and inexpensive production, HFCS enables packaged foods to stay fresh longer and gives baked goods a flaky texture. Foods that contain HFCS are also less likely to crystallize when cooled, making them less susceptible to freezer burn. Sports drinks, bread, peanut butter, yogurt, canned vegetables, fruit juice, ice cream, soda, candy, and cake—all contain hefty amounts of HFCS.

Fructose is everywhere. Our systems are loaded with it. An unaware eater can have fructose in every bite of every meal, leading to sky-high fructose levels. Our systems were not designed to deal with the amount of fructose that we eat today.

# THE GIFTS OF FRUCTOSE:
# AN ALCOHOLIC'S LIVER, A JACKED
# METABOLISM, AND NEVER FEELING FULL

As packaged foods became more prevalent, fructose-rich sweeteners started to replace sucrose (table sugar). Not only is fructose in the form of HFCS sweeter and cheaper than sucrose, but it was originally thought to have health benefits as well. Consumers and health experts loved the short-term effect that fructose has on blood sugar. While glucose goes straight into the bloodstream, fructose goes to the liver, thus preventing glucose spikes. Moreover, fructose in the absence of glucose reduces blood sugar. By simulating hepatic glucokinase, an enzyme that helps metabolism, the liver is turned into a glucose sponge and soaks up extra glucose in the bloodstream. Everyone was happy: both sugar addicts and health experts finally agreed on an acceptable sugar. Fructose was instantly dubbed the healthier alternative. But the accolade had been bestowed too soon.

> **Sugar is a sometimes drug and should only be used recreationally.**

Fructose has its own drawbacks. It may not spike glucose and insulin levels, but in large amounts, it forces the liver into overdrive. When the liver is too full of fructose, the sugar turns into fat that stays in the liver, where there's little chance for it to be turned into energy. If you ever want to burn that fat, your body has to be running extremely low on glucose. There's little chance of that happening on today's carb-heavy diet.

Forty years ago, fructose was deemed the most *lypogenic* carbohydrate—the carbohydrate that turns to fat most readily. Clever marketing, increased sweetness (as fruits are selectively bred and hybridized), prolonged shelf life, and year-round availability have helped us forget this fact.

The bad consequences of fructose go beyond its propensity to turn into fat. Fructose triggers a domino effect in the body that causes a change in metabolism. Under the influence of fructose, muscles and fat become resistant to insulin, which in turn influences how nutrients are stored. The result? You get fatter.

The litany of detrimental side effects continues. Although packed with calories, fructose won't tell your brain that your body is full. The hypothalamus is the appetite control center in the brain—your internal nutrient counter. Hormones serve as messengers to tell the brain whether the body is hungry or full. Depending on which hormones are circulating (insulin, leptin, cholecystokinin, or ghrelin), you are told when to eat, when to keep eating, and when to put down the fork. Fructose, however, does not stimulate any of these "enough-to-eat" hormones. (See page 61 for more on these hormones.) This is why you can eat fruit all day long and never feel full.

Fructose is far from being the sugar savior it was once crowned. It breeds fat in the liver, leaves you ravenous, causes insulin resistance, and results in hyperinsulinemia (a condition in which there is excess insulin compared to what is expected based on glucose levels). Elevated insulin directly inhibits the metabolism of stored fat. So, with fructose, you eat more, get fat, and then stay fat because it's harder to dip into energy stores. It's a real lose-lose (or perhaps a weight gain-gain!) situation.

## WHAT YOU CAN DO ABOUT SUGAR FOR OPTIMAL HEALTH

**Eliminate all processed foods containing fructose from your diet**, including condiments and juice, also known as liquid fructose.

**Avoid the habit of eating fruit as a daily snack** just because it's convenient. Stock your pantry with easy on-the-go proteins, like tuna in a pouch or beef jerky. Having healthy, convenient alternatives will help you avoid the fruit bowl.

**Use the tastiness of real fruit sparingly** to enhance dishes with flavor and variety.

## Chapter 3

# HORMONES: MANAGING THE BODY'S TRAFFIC SIGNALS

## Making hormones work for you to avoid fat storage, maximize satisfaction from food, and use stress to make you stronger, not weaker

## HORMONES:

## THE BODY'S COMMUNICATION NETWORK

The human body is made up of many different systems: circulatory, digestive, muscular, nervous, respiratory, reproductive, urinary, lymphatic, immune, and more. While each system has a different function, they all have to work together toward a common goal—keeping you alive. To get on the same page, they communicate with hormones. Hormones are chemical messengers sent through the blood to tell the rest of the body what's going on and how to behave.

When hormones are mentioned, most people think of the sex hormones, testosterone and estrogen. But various other types of hormones circulate through the body at any given time, and their levels are affected by the environment. What you eat, how you sleep, how you work out, and your levels of stress all affect the messages your body circulates. If you want to keep yourself looking like a Greek god or goddess, you need to make sure that your hormones are sending out the right marching orders. Not enough sleep, too much stress, and too little exercise can have adverse effects on hormonal signaling and, ultimately, your waistline.

# INSULIN:
## THE HORMONE OF UTMOST IMPORTANCE

The body's system of hormones can seem complicated. But for one hormone in particular, insulin, it's worth the extra effort to understand how the foods you eat affect your body.

When excess glucose is circulating in the bloodstream, insulin directs that glucose to one of the body's three storage banks—the muscles, liver, or, if those two are full, fat cells (adipose tissues). Insulin activates one of the keys (the lipoprotein lipase) that opens up fat cells' doors to store excess glucose, amino acids, and even lipids (fat) in the event of famine. When opened, the fat cells transform glucose to fat for long-term storage.

In other words, insulin helps make you fat. High levels of insulin in your blood mean that more glucose is being shuttled into the adipose cells to be transformed into fat. Low levels of insulin mean fewer glucose-to-fat transformations. Unfortunately, the diet recommended by the USDA and other experts is high in carbohydrates, especially fructose, which results in insulin resistance coupled with high glucose levels in the blood. High glucose sends insulin soaring and waistlines bulging. If you control your insulin, you will feel terrific and be lean into your twilight years.

# INSULIN AND GLUCAGON: THE HORMONE TAG TEAM THAT KEEPS ENERGY FLOWING

Glucose is a cell's main energy source. Without it, cells are like cars without gas: they won't run. The pancreas monitors levels of glucose in the blood to make sure that your cells are never running on empty, whether you are stuffed, starving, sleeping, or active. Responding to glucose levels, the pancreas produces two types of hormones, insulin and glucagon.

When glucose levels are high, the beta cells of the pancreas produce insulin. This hormone circulates in the blood, directing the storage of glucose in muscle, liver, and fat cells. Insulin reduces the concentration of glucose in the bloodstream.

When blood glucose levels are low, such as between meals or during sleep, the alpha cells of the pancreas produce glucagon. This hormone directs the liver to transform glycogen (the long polysaccharide form of stored glucose) into glucose, which is then released into the blood. Glucose levels rise.

Together, insulin and glucagon work to maintain a steady supply of glucose—that is, energy—to the cells and, most important, to the brain. These hormones send marching orders to the cells and tell them whether energy should be stored or released.

## INSULIN: GET THE CONCEPT OR GET FAT

Back to carbohydrates. When you eat carbs, especially simple ones that explode quickly in your system, glucose is quickly released into your blood. As glucose levels rise, the pancreas receives a signal to secrete insulin. Insulin causes cells in the liver, muscles, and fat tissues to take glucose from the blood and convert it to glycogen for storage. Think of glycogen as a storage system for the body to easily access energy later.

Nature designed the human body to work best when fed the natural foods available in the environment of long ago. Nature's foods provide a slow, steady release of energy. The carb-rich foods we eat today contain excessive amounts of glucose (as well as fructose) that explode quickly in the blood. More insulin is needed to control blood glucose levels, and it is hard for the body to keep up with the demands on insulin production. The demand is so high that the beta cells, the insulin factories of the pancreas, have to work in overdrive. The pancreas tries its best to increase insulin supply to meet the rise in demand, but under this kind of stress, over long periods, the beta cells get tired and can no longer keep up the pace. Exhausted, these overworked cells suffer from early death, known as *apoptosis*. The pancreas can no longer produce enough insulin to control glucose levels, which can lead to type 2 diabetes.

When the pancreas gets fatigued, so do cells. Hormones are like nagging parents: when they are constantly telling the cells to do the same thing over and over again, the cells simply tune them out, like rebellious children. When you have consistently high levels of insulin circulating through your system, your cells stop listening to their marching orders. In order to be heard, the insulin message has to get louder—requiring even more work of the already overworked pancreas. This vicious cycle is called *insulin resistance*. In an insulin-resistant person, the cells need more insulin to do the same job. Gone unchecked, insulin resistance is another cause of type 2 diabetes.

Still think that this insulin warning does not apply to you? Let's try another angle: fat. High levels of insulin increase the amount of time your body stores fat and decrease the time available to burn it. Because of this inverse relationship with insulin, increased carbs in your diet not only make you fat but also make you stay fat, even if you are eating fewer calories than you need.

Carbohydrates are broken down into glucose, and glucose triggers insulin. Monitoring your carb consumption is more important than following a trendy diet. It is a tool to stay ahead of your health. Your insulin factory will not be in overdrive, and your cells will remain sensitive to the hormone messengers that let your body know when you need energy. Furthermore, you will avoid both short- and long-term negative health consequences.

# HOW WELL THE CELLS LISTEN: INSULIN SENSITIVITY

How quickly glucose is cleared from your blood is important. When your system is working optimally and your cells are listening to the hormone insulin, excess glucose is removed quickly. This means insulin is doing its job: taking the fuel available and sending it into cells (muscle, liver, or fat) for immediate use or storage. Consistently high glucose levels, however, tire out your pancreas (your insulin factory) and dull the cells' ability to listen to the message insulin sends. As a result of this communication breakdown, insulin doesn't perform its job as quickly or effectively.

The result: glucose is not dealt with properly. Instead of being transported into the cells to be used for energy, it remains in the bloodstream, making mischief everywhere from the skin to DNA.

When glucose has a chance to hang out in the blood instead of being filed away, it can stick to proteins and form *advanced glycation end products* (AGEs). AGEs do exactly what the acronym implies: they age you. Having too much glucose circulating makes you look older faster. The glycation of collagen is implicated in the formation of wrinkled skin.

The effects of excess circulating glucose are more than skin deep. When excess glucose is processed, a by-product called a *reactive oxygen species* (ROS) is created. To remain harmless, ROS must be neutralized by antioxidants. However, we eat so much sugar and so few nutrient-dense foods that our bodies no longer have the antioxidants to neutralize these little devils. Overwhelming the body's defense system, ROSs are free to damage cells, including DNA. Long-term exposure to oxidative stress is involved in many diseases, including Alzheimer's, Parkinson's, and chronic fatigue syndrome, as well as accelerated aging. It's especially hard on cells with slow turnover, such as those in the joints and eyes, and can therefore affect mobility and vision.

You want a diet that keeps your pancreas out of overdrive and your cells listening to insulin. You don't want too much insulin—the fat maker—around. If you are smart about your carbohydrate consumption, you can avoid many of the negative effects of high glucose levels. Choose slow-burning fuels such as greens, broccoli, and cauliflower. They give you the energy you need without a rush of glucose through your system.

### NORMAL CELL

- Insulin is doing its job, allowing glucose to flow into cells when there is excess in the system.

- Glucose is utilized effectively by the cell, which goes about its business with energy steadily coming in and, depending on cell type, going out.

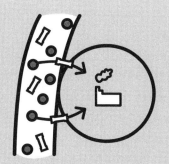

### INSULIN-RESISTANT CELL

- Cells require additional insulin to store glucose, sending the pancreas into overdrive.

- Some glucose cannot make it into the cells and instead globs around the cells, causing oxidation problems.

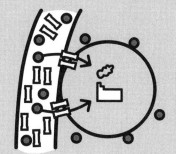

 GLUCOSE  INSULIN

# BEYOND INSULIN:

# AN INTRODUCTION TO CORTISOL

While controlling insulin is paramount for long-term health and is easily within your power, insulin is not the only chemical messenger that affects your waistline. Stress causes more than just annoyance; it also triggers the hormones adrenaline and cortisol, which affect how your body stores and releases fat.

Cortisol is an important "get-moving" hormone, enabling you to get up and about after a long overnight fast. It prepares your body to deal with whatever is in the environment as soon as you open your sleepy eyes. When cortisol circulates, it tells cells to release glucose. This glucose is used to fuel muscles and to jump-start your body until you can provide it with energy in the form of food. Thus your body produces cortisol in a natural cycle. Throughout the night, it ramps up cortisol production. When you wake up, cortisol is naturally at its highest. During the day, cortisol levels decline until they reach their lowest point in the early evening.

Adrenaline is another hormone that signals the body to release glucose. Adrenaline is called to action to help meet physical demands in a dangerous world. It evolved to alert the body to flee or fight when the environment is hostile—a brilliant adaptation. It arms cells with loads of fuel in the form of glucose to respond to a threat, whether by running away fast or fighting hard. This glucose surge makes the brain think and react intelligently and gives the muscles energy to perform well. Under these conditions, even fats and proteins are quickly metabolized into energy. When faced with a threat, the circumstance—feast or famine—doesn't matter. Adrenaline triggers the release of energy (glucose) into the blood to help you emerge victorious.

In addition to triggering cells to pour glucose into the blood, cortisol and adrenaline tell the body when to store or release fat. In the hunter-gatherer world for which the human body was designed, stress meant fighting or running from predators. In terms of immediate survival, running from predators ranked higher on the to-do list than eating, and a human on the run couldn't stop for a snack. So, thinking that it is doing you a favor, stress triggers your body to hold onto fat as just-in-case storage.

Adrenaline served people well in a world where a saber-tooth tiger could attack or woolly mammoths could stampede. However, the functional role of acute stress (adrenaline) in the caveman world has morphed into unhealthy chronic stress (cortisol) today. As soon as you walk out the door, you are faced with situations that put your body on alert: A car cuts you off. Crises arise at the office. A typical day can be made up of ceaseless stressors, and the body perceives each of these encounters as a threat. Accordingly, it keeps cortisol levels high and fat-burning low.

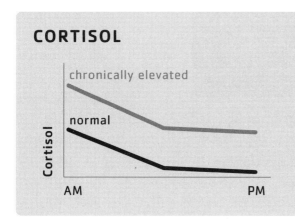

# TOO MUCH EXERCISE ADDS TO STRESS (AND FAT STORAGE)

Challenging the body in the right way can be healthy. Increased demands on the body call for a momentary bump in cortisol, which dissipates within an hour. When you choose the right type of exercise, this momentary bump can fuel activity that stimulates your muscles and bones to become stronger. It can also result in an overall reduction of stress post-activity.

However, your body reads too great a challenge as a stressor. To your body, excess exercise is the equivalent of running from lions. Running from lions is stressful (read: your body produces more cortisol). While the human body was designed to deal with bouts of stress, it was not designed to deal with chronically high levels. While you think you are doing yourself a favor by burning calories with your daily one-hour treadmill session, your body thinks it is doing you a bigger favor by holding tight to the emergency fat fund. The work you are putting in may be counteracted by the cortisol circulating in your system as a result of your overzealousness.

> Too many extended cardio workouts and metabolic beatdowns make your body think you are running from lions.

High levels of stress from daily life compounded by constant intense exercise can be a recipe for disaster. If over the course of years you consistently overtrain—always pushing for maximum effort or working until your body fails—you can put your cortisol factories into overdrive. Gone unchecked, the adrenal glands, which produce cortisol, become overworked and can no longer keep up with demand. This is called *adrenal fatigue*.

# TIPS FOR MAKING CORTISOL WORK FOR YOU

**Avoid foods that spike blood sugar.** Fast rises in glucose are followed by crashes. When blood sugar dips below baseline, your body worries that it is starving. In response, it revs into gear with a stress response to get glucose to cells fast. Eat fats and proteins instead, which fill you up by producing the right hormonal cues without the stress of the roller coaster ride.

**Avoid consistent cardio workouts.** Too many extended cardio workouts and metabolic beatdowns make your body think you are running from lions. Running from lions stresses the body, and when this stress is chronic, it causes the body to conserve potential energy by storing fat. How much exercise is too much? That depends on you and what your body can tolerate. Check out the tests on pages 173 and 180 to help determine what is right for you.

**Sleep in a dark room.** Too much ambient light while sleeping does not allow the proper reset of hormones at night.

**Avoid bright lights before bed.** Stay away from computer and TV screens and other bright lights. Bright lights late at night make the body think summer. Summer means winter is coming. Winter means less food. Less food in the future means the body needs to store more fat now.

**Beware of super-low carbs if you are an athlete.** In order to increase the breakdown of proteins and fats into fuel, the process of gluconeogenesis upregulates cortisol. This means extra stress on the body. Athletes who train hard benefit from including a source of quality carbohydrates, such as sweet potatoes, in their diet.

**Meditate to de-stress.** Modern life is busy and full of demands. Take time to slow down, breathe deeply, and be present. Small efforts to reduce stress levels in the body can go a long way.

When your hormone factories are worn out, your body is not helped by challenges such as moderate exercise. You no longer see gains in performance, and you feel tired, sluggish, and unmotivated. More time at the gym won't help you get over this fatigued state. The only thing that can help you recover is rest.

## THE SIGNAL OF SATISFACTION: "ENOUGH-TO-EAT" HORMONES

Fullness of the stomach does not signal that the body is satisfied. This is why you can be stuffed and still feel compelled to eat. Instead, hormones, the body's communication tools, signal you to eat or stop eating.

Hormones are made in a variety of locations throughout the body. Insulin is made in the pancreas. Other hormones are produced in the thyroid, hypothalamus, and reproductive organs. The biggest hormone factory is the digestive system. From beginning to end, your gut is one large endocrine system. It is a complex sensory tool that passes information about what is going on throughout the body.

The foods you eat affect the messages that circulate in your blood. Your gut communicates to your body the answers to questions like: Is it time to eat or stop eating? Is food abundant in the environment or is it scarce? Is it time to store up for winter?

> Satiated describes a state of feeling satisfied and no longer compelled to eat. When you consume protein and fat, the desire to eat goes away. When you consume carbs, the stomach can be full but not satisfied, leading you to eat more.

Hormones produced in the gut and throughout the body regulate your appetite according to the relationship between food intake and metabolism. They tell your body when to eat more (the hormone ghrelin) and when to stop eating (hormones such as leptin, peptide YY, cholecystokinin, glucagon-like peptide 1, and oxyntomodulin).

When it comes to regulating energy, most of us have a good sense of when we need to eat. When to stop is a more challenging problem. The key to putting the fork down is in the "enough-to-eat" hormones, especially leptin. In today's standard diet, the messages of these hormones are lost in translation. However, when you eat what you are designed to eat, the message of when to stop comes through loud and clear.

## WHEN IT COMES TO FOOD, THINK SATISFIED, NOT FULL

Imagine a pot. When empty, it has room for something to be put in it. When full, it has no more capacity. When applied to the body, "empty" means hungry, and "full" is supposed to mean not hungry. Volume is what fills up the pot, so we assume that volume is also what fills our stomachs and signals us to stop eating. But it has happened to the best of us: we still feel hungry even after we have finished a large meal. If our bellies are full, why are we still hungry?

The term *full* has the wrong connotation; it should be replaced with *satisfied*. Satisfied describes a state of feeling satiated and no longer compelled to eat. The desire to eat more is gone.

Satisfaction does not have to do with the volume of food occupying the stomach. You can feel satisfied and not be "full." Conversely, you can be full without being satisfied. If satisfied is the state you want to achieve, how do you get there? Carbs just fill the pot. Instead, eat foods that satisfy, proteins and fats.

> The key to putting the fork down is in the "enough-to-eat" hormones.

When you eat the right foods, the "enough-to-eat" hormones are produced in your gut. Protein and fat stimulate hormone production and help you feel satiated. When you eat these foods, your body gets busy processing the nutrients for immediate needs and short-term storage. Foods such as grains and sugars do not produce the same response in the "enough-to-eat" hormones, leading you to serve yourself unneeded seconds.

What you eat is not the only factor that affects the "enough-to-eat" hormones. When you are stressed, your body hedges its bets by preparing for the worst-case scenario, ensuring that you have enough stored energy to face a potential threat. Thus you are stimulated by stress to eat more and store more. This stress can be a result of the typical demands of modern life. It can also be caused by something as simple as one night of bad sleep. When you don't get enough sleep, your appetite is seriously affected, triggering your body to reduce the production of leptin and increase ghrelin. This is why you eat more and don't stop when full when you are tired.

## LEPTIN RESISTANCE AND
## THE DANGERS OF NEVER FEELING FULL

In addition to being produced in the gut, "enough-to-eat" hormones are secreted by adipose (fat) tissue. When you eat large amounts of the wrong foods—bad carbs, sugar, grains—excess sugars are sent to fat cells for long-term storage. As you stuff yourself with these unhealthy foods, the rush for storage space becomes so great that the fat cells find themselves in danger of failing to keep up with the demand. They produce elevated leptin to tell the body to stop sending nutrients their way. The more fat you have, the louder the leptin message. Under normal conditions, this would make you feel satisfied and stop eating, but excess leptin can negate its own effect.

Moderate amounts of "enough-to-eat" hormones help you feel comfortably satisfied. However, in the case of leptin, more of a good thing is not better. A modern diet of highly processed carbs, chronic stress, and a lack of adequate sleep combine to result in high levels of leptin. Just as your cells stop listening when too much insulin is present, your body stops listening when too much leptin is present.

With chronic exposure, the body no longer hears the "I'm full" message. Over time, leptin cannot pass the blood-brain barrier. As a result, the "I'm full" message doesn't make it to the control center—and you find yourself eating and eating and never feeling satisfied. Even worse, thinking that you need more food, your brain compels you to eat more. This vicious cycle makes weight loss difficult.

> **You are stimulated by stress to eat more and store more.**

## HEARING THE "ENOUGH-TO-EAT" MESSENGERS LOUD AND CLEAR

The foods you eat affect the hormones that control your appetite. You need to eat the foods that generate the right amount of "enough-to-eat" hormones to make you stop eating, rather than the foods that produce so much of these hormones that your brain tunes the message out.

Here are some tips to make "enough-to-eat" hormones work for you, not against you:

- Eat proteins and fats, which stimulate "enough-to-eat" hormones.
- Avoid foods that cause spikes in sugar and a subsequent overproduction of leptin.

- Get adequate sleep.

- Work to lose the fat that overproduces leptin, causing dangerously high levels that lead to leptin resistance.

- Avoid grazing. Eating constantly can elevate leptin levels abnormally.

## MORE THAN A LUXURY: THE IMPORTANCE OF SLEEP

*The Guinness Book of World Records* tracks all sorts of crazy achievements, including freefalling, sword-swallowing, and glass-eating. However, one world record will no longer be found in this tome of human achievement—sleep deprivation. Why did *Guinness* stop recording this fact? Because a lack of sleep is downright dangerous.

More than a luxury, sleep is an essential biological function. Without it the body can't function optimally. The problem? Most people don't get enough sleep. Here are some compelling reasons to get more shut-eye.

**Sleep helps regulate appetite.** When you don't get adequate sleep, your hormones become imbalanced. Your level of leptin (the "stop eating" hormone) decreases by 18 percent. At the same time, your level of ghrelin (the "eat" hormone) increases by 28 percent. When you are sleep deprived, you have a greater appetite and eat more. Not only are you hungrier, but you also crave high-carbohydrate foods.

**Sleep affects your decision-making.** One night of poor sleep changes the brain's ability to function. The prefrontal cortex, which controls logical reasoning, shuts down. The result: you are no longer capable of thinking through your decisions. Choices like going to the gym and eating healthy foods become more difficult. Fatigue is apt to lead you down the wrong path.

**Sleep changes the way your body processes sugar.** If you eat right and don't get enough sleep, all your hard work is for naught. Lack of sleep affects the way the body processes sugar and changes your body's glucose metabolism. Insulin production increases, and your body stores fat more easily. Just a few days of sleep deprivation can lead the body to enter a prediabetic state.

**Sleep affects performance.** Children who sleep more score higher on IQ tests. For adults, sleep affects the ability to complete simple and complex tasks, both mental and physical. One night without sleep leaves you performing as if you were legally drunk, with a blood alcohol level of 0.08.

**Sleep affects stress.** Cortisol is the body's main stress hormone. While it has some important day-to-day functions, this messenger can get carried away with its charge: to protect you in times of danger. Adequate sleep is required to control this hormone so that it works for you, not against you. When you don't sleep enough, your body produces more cortisol. To ensure survival, cortisol signals the cells to store fat and burn muscle. All that wasted gym time! In addition, high levels of this stress hormone make you ravenous, so you eat more.

## WHAT YOU CAN DO ABOUT HORMONES FOR OPTIMAL HEALTH

**Keep your pancreas out of overdrive** by minimizing your consumption of foods that cause quick rises in blood sugar.

**Eat foods that increase insulin sensitivity,** such as cinnamon.

**Prevent your body from going into stress mode** by eating on a regular schedule and not skipping meals in times of stress.

**Intermittent fasting can be beneficial,** but never fast during periods of stress.

## Chapter 4

# INFLAMMATION: WHEN FOOD BECOMES FOE

How food fosters rebellion in the gut, microbes protect the fortresses, and what you eat can be your biggest ally in health

## THE DOUBLE-EDGED
## SWORD OF INFLAMMATION

Inflammation is an important part of the healing process. When you sprain your ankle, it swells. This reaction is the result of your body's healing agents mobilizing and rushing to fix the problem. Most people think only of this visible, acute reaction when they think of inflammation—the redness, swelling, and tenderness. However, the inflammation you can't see, present in the blood, has more influence on your health and waistline.

Acute inflammation is a good thing that helps heal the body. But if the body is always in healing mode, it experiences *chronic* inflammation, which is damaging. When your body experiences nonstop inflammation, it is constantly fighting invaders. The relentless siege taxes the body's defenses. While it is fighting on one front, resources are not available to fight new threats like disease and infection, and you get sick more often.

One of the most common sources of chronic inflammation is food. When you eat the wrong foods, chronic inflammation can start in your digestive system and move into the bloodstream and through the entire body.

Inflammation can be likened to emergency vehicles that go out to fight problems. Your veins and arteries are the roads that take these vehicles around the body. Constantly bombarding your system with heavy equipment and nonstop traffic wears it out. These highways—your veins and arteries—become less elastic, and the road system gets smaller. Chronic inflammation makes you age faster. It also damages your DNA, making it more prone to replication errors that increase the chances that cells may become cancerous. Finally, chronic inflammation increases the risk of diabetes, high blood sugar, and weight gain.

The brain needs glucose to do its job. Inflammation in the intestine lowers efficiency and prevents glucose from getting to hungry cells. The result? Your body feels a nutritional deficit and tells you to eat more. To feel better quickly, you are compelled to eat bad foods that can be processed quickly. These bad foods cause more inflammation, perpetuating the vicious cycle.

Some causes of acute inflammation are beyond your control, such as the body fighting bacteria or viruses or healing from injury. However, chronic inflammation can be controlled. Avoid foods that cause inflammation, and load up on foods that help fight it.

| Anti-Inflammatory | Moderately Inflammatory | Egregiously Inflammatory |
|---|---|---|
| Broccoli | Potatoes | Wheat |
| Brussels sprouts | Legumes (beans, peas, lentils) | Rye |
| Cabbage | | Barley |
| Kale | Corn | Oats |
| Sweet potatoes | Rice | Sugar (white, brown, fructose) |
| Grapefruit | Watermelon | |
| Berries | Bananas | Alcohol |
| Herbs | Honey | Artificial food additives |
| | Quinoa | |
| Almonds | Canola oil | Fried foods |
| Walnuts | Vegetable oil | Peanuts |
| Olive oil | | Trans fats |
| Fish oil | | |
| Coconut oil | | |
| Chicken (pasture-raised) | Beef and poultry (grain-fed) | Soy |
| | | Tofu |
| Beef (grass-fed) | Dairy | Processed meats (salami, bologna) |
| Fish (wild- or line-caught) | | |
| Omega-3 eggs | | |

# FOOD AS FRIEND OR FOE

The body needs to keep the bad stuff out to be safe from invaders that harm and destroy. At the same time, supplies from the outside world are needed to keep the body going. To get these nutrients, it is necessary to allow some exposure to destructive elements. To deal with this problem, the body separates incoming material in the gut into food friends and food foes. Food friends are needed reinforcements that fuel and replenish the body. Food foes weaken your defenses and cause damage.

Food friends and food foes are separated in the small intestine for their different journeys. The small intestine acts as a checkpoint on the road, letting the good nutrients through to the bloodstream and hungry cells and turning aside the bad stuff, which keeps moving along its way to be eliminated from the body.

When the small intestine is overrun with bad food, the body mobilizes to keep the bad stuff out of the bloodstream. Inflammation comes to the rescue, fortifying the small intestine to prevent the absorption of toxins into the bloodstream. Inflamed surface cells in the intestine cut the absorption area from about 2 million square centimeters to 2,000 square centimeters. But less absorption area for the bad stuff also means that there is less absorption area for the good nutrients the body needs. The body's overzealous attempt to protect against food foes also can cause injury. Innocent, helpful cells are caught in the crossfire, preventing them from transporting good foods.

Unable to get the needed supplies through the inflamed intestines, your body tells you that you ate the wrong food through stomachaches, gas, diarrhea, cramps, and bloating. You feel groggy and have less energy. You often don't understand the message and, as a result, you do not heed the warning.

Inflammation from food foes does not stop in the small intestine. Despite the body's best efforts to keep the bad stuff moving toward elimination, food foes sometimes slip through the checkpoint and enter the bloodstream. Once again, the body sends inflammation emergency vehicles through the bloodstream to deal with the threat.

# UNDER SIEGE:
## SNEAKY FOODS AND THEIR EFFECTS

Like humans, plants have evolved to reproduce more effectively. Different plants have different strategies. Some, like fruits, have developed a "give a little, get a little" strategy. Fruits give critters a scrumptious, energy-rich flesh. In exchange for this delicious treat, the plants expect some seeds to be carried to new places and deposited in fertile packets to propagate and grow. It's a mutually beneficial arrangement.

Wild grasses—the predecessors of wheat, rye, oats, barley, millet, and rice—developed a different strategy. Their seeds need to reach maturity before spreading to the wind. To deter small rodents from chowing down before the seeds had a chance to mature, grains developed self-defense mechanisms. These self-defense mechanisms cause irritation during digestion, making small critters sick and deterring them from demolishing the plant's ability to reproduce. The grass's defenses worked, at least for small animals. When larger animals started to belly up to the grain buffet, however, those self-defense mechanisms no longer had the same level of success in driving them away—but they still cause problems in the digestive system.

During human digestion, grains are broken down into a variety of proteins, including some called *lectins*. While the body is trying hard to keep food foes out, lectins disguise harmful molecules. The disguise, a type of molecular mimicry, makes the body think that food foes are friends. The body lets these molecules into the bloodstream, where they can bind to almost any tissue and wreak havoc. Different grains and legumes contain different lectins: soybeans contain SBA, peanuts PNA, and kidney beans PHA. One of the nastier forms of lectin is wheat germ agglutinin (WGA), found most commonly in the wheat kernel. These large protein/carbohydrate hybrids are not broken down in digestion. When soaked or cooked, the effects of these lectins are minimized. However, wheat gluten—specifically, the gliadin protein in gluten—does not break down in cooking. Gliadin is a prime food foe.

Once the enemy combatants breach gut barrios and are circulating, the body figures out the disguise and sends an emergency response team to fight with inflammation. But there's a problem: lectins look similar to the body's good proteins. When the emergency crews are fighting, they can mistake good guys for bad guys and hose them down in the confusion. For many people, this results in high levels of inflammation. Extreme cases result in autoimmune disease, such as rheumatoid arthritis or multiple sclerosis.

> **The body tries hard to keep food foes out. Disguised as food friends, lectins breach the body's defenses and enter the bloodstream, where they wreak havoc.**

The effects of these large protein hybrids don't stop there. As large, unauthorized proteins glom onto the gut lining, they break down the defenses and cause intestinal permeability, or "leaky gut." Partially digested food spills into the bloodstream. The more breaches in the gut, the more food sensitivities you develop. The body also becomes less capable of extracting needed sugars, proteins, and fats from food friends.

# GETTING YOUR GUT BACK ON TRACK:
## LEARNING TO LISTEN TO THE MESSAGE

Your body doesn't have a megaphone. It speaks subtly, communicating through bellyaches, diarrhea, stomach cramps, and fatigue. But since most people consume inflammatory food foes (wheat, oats, barley, rice, and corn) daily, these messages are ignored. Other times a diagnosis can't be definitively determined, and patients are given an unspecific verdict of "irritable bowel." While silently suffering internally, we see around us more cases of obesity, arthritis, heart disease, and autoimmune disease. One culprit is raging, unseen inflammation.

Cleaning up your diet repairs the damage and gets your system in working order again. People who embrace a Paleo diet (which cuts out food foes) are rewarded by feeling good. Try a Paleo diet for a month and see if you look, feel, and perform better. See page 199 for the Squeaky Clean Paleo sample meal plan.

If you want to cheat on a Paleo diet, cheat the smart way. Know how foods fight back and which ones pack the most harmful punch. Wheat gluten is one of the most harmful. Gluten is bad for you when consumed on a daily basis, but even one cheat meal containing gluten can cause damage it could take your body a week to recover from, depending on your gut and immune function. So when the time comes to cheat, choose other grains and avoid gluten altogether.

> **Your body doesn't have a megaphone. It speaks subtly.**

# THE GARDEN IN YOUR GUT:
# AN INTRODUCTION TO THE MICROBIOME

Your body's fortress, the gut, is not the only system you have to protect you from enemy invaders that can end up in your bloodstream, causing systemic inflammation. In a healthy gut, a population of microbes works to help process beneficial nutrients, neutralize toxins, and protect the gut fortifications. But not all microbes are good. Like food friends and food foes, some microbes help you, bolstering digestion, fortifications, and health, while others hurt you, causing breaches in the gut that lead to increased gut permeability and toxicity loads.

The body is more than just the cells that make it up. Microbes cover your hands, skin, ears, and nose. They also live inside you—in your stomach, intestines, and lungs. While the human body contains 10 trillion cells, it has ten times that number of microbes. In fact, there is more bacterial DNA in your body than human DNA. You are about 1 percent human cells and 99 percent bacteria.

Bacteria get a lot of bad press and are rarely celebrated for the good they do. One good bacteria, for example—*Staphylococcus epidermis*—releases toxins that kill pathogens and sends immune signals that speed healing. A healthy gut flora also helps neutralize toxins from the foods you eat and from pathogenic microbes. In some cases, the cell's wall of helpful bacteria absorbs many carcinogenic substances.

Bacteria are not just passive riders; they are active participants in keeping the body alive and healthy. These single-cell organisms have coevolved with us and perform many essential tasks. Your system relies heavily on these microbes to help break up starches and other tough molecules, dismantle toxins in your food, and build essential vitamins. They even affect how your body absorbs and stores the food you eat. With the wrong microbes, the body absorbs more fatty acids and carbohydrates and ultimately stores more of what you eat as fat. Bacteria can also trigger hormonal signals like the production of insulin (leading to insulin resistance—see page 53) and cause inflammation of the hypothalamus (leading to leptin resistance—see page 62). Microbes are the front line of defense for the immune system. A healthy ecosystem of helpful bacteria support a healthy immune system; together, good bacteria and the gut's immune system—gut-associated lymphoid tissue (GALT)—protect the body from invasion.

## THE RICH MICROBIAL ECOSYSTEM

While it is sometimes possible to identify individual bacteria and what they do, it is not just particular bacteria that are good for you; it's the ecosystem as a whole. Like a rainforest or coral reef, the gut flora is a diverse and thriving community of life. Individual species are linked through energy flows and nutrient cycles. Individual microbes, good and bad, compete for space. In a healthy population, good microbes keep the bad microbes in check and keep populations under control. But the balance of power in the gut is constantly changing.

Microbial diversity varies greatly from person to person. Some people have healthy, thriving ecosystems, and others do not. Healthy gut flora starts early in life. Before birth, the walls of a mother's birth canal are populated by the flora that live in her gut. When a baby travels through the birth canal, she is exposed to the mother's healthy or unhealthy gut flora. After birth, the first couple of weeks are imperative for developing a thriving ecosystem of helpful bacteria. One of the most important ways a child is exposed to healthy gut flora is through breast milk. Up to 60 percent of breast milk is microbial, which gives the child exposure to the bacterial diversity she needs to survive and thrive.

Disadvantaged from the start are babies delivered by C-section, babies who are not breastfed, and children whose mothers have to take antibiotics during breastfeeding. Their systems lack exposure to vital microbial diversity. Such lack of diversity can lead to unbalanced microbial populations, resulting in increased toxicity in the blood, systemic inflammation of the gut, digestive disorders, poor absorption of nutrients in food, irritable bowel syndrome (IBS), finicky eating, and a host of other problems down the line.

After the microbial base is planted early in life, the ecosystem continues to evolve. Diet is one of the main factors that affect microbial diversity and your microbe ecosystem. Eating nature's foods results in a healthy and robust population of beneficial microbes in your gut, encouraging a well-functioning system. In contrast, if you eat a diet full of highly processed foods, the ecosystem in your gut does not get the helpful microorganisms. In addition, bad microbes like *Candida albicans* thrive on refined carbohydrates. With more resources available to them, they grow and take over more than their share of the system.

Internal and external factors change the types of microbes that thrive in the gut. Small shifts are inevitable as a result of diet and lifestyle. But catastrophic shifts can occur in the ecosystem, such as when taking penicillins, tetracyclines, and other antibiotics. These shifts can kill off whole species of microbes and leave entire niches open to be filled by bad microbes, yeasts, and fungi.

If your digestive system is out of whack, you can usually restore the natural balance relatively easily. If a catastrophic change occurs, however, as would result from taking multiple rounds of antibiotics, you need to work hard to rebuild a fragile ecosystem.

## IN THE GUT ARE THREE TYPES OF FLORA

**Essential or beneficial:** In a healthy person, this group is the largest and most important. These bacteria aid in the processing and digestion of food. The main types in this group include *Bifidobacterium, Lactobacillus*, strains of *E. coli, Peptostreptococcus*, and *Enterococcus*.

**Opportunistic:** In a healthy gut, around 500 species of microbes are tightly controlled by healthy populations. If these microbes get out of control, however, they can cause serious health problems. They include *Bacteroides, Peptococcus, Staphylococcus, Streptococcus, Bacillus, Clostriadium*, yeasts, enterobacteria (for instance, *Proteus, Klebsiella, Citrobacter*), *Fusobacterium, Eubacterium*, and many others.

**Transitional:** These are the microbes that we ingest in foods and beverages. When the gut is working well, they do no harm. If the gut flora is not functioning properly, however, these microbes can lead to disease.

# THE IMPORTANCE OF A HEALTHY MICRO-BIOME TO PROTECT AGAINST LEAKY GUT

Having a healthy microbiome is key to keeping the body's fortresses strong so that they can efficiently let the good in and keep the bad out. When the gut is healthy, it is covered in a bacterial layer of protection. This physical barrier is the first line of defense against undigested foods, invaders, toxins, and parasites. In addition to lining the gut walls, these helpful microorganisms work against invasive pathogenic microorganisms by producing antibiotic-like substances, antifungals, and antiviral substances that dissolve the membranes of viruses and bacteria. They also engage the immune system to deal with unwelcome guests before they make it past the fortresses. Without this beneficial shield, the body's fortresses are more likely to be weakened and broken, allowing inflammation-causing substances into the bloodstream.

The right microbial diversity not only protects the gut walls with a physical barrier but also lowers toxicity in the gut. Your gut is exposed to a lot of toxicity from the foods you eat, as well as from the toxins created by pathogenic microbes. A healthy gut flora is able to neutralize nitrates, phenols, and other toxic substances. The cell walls of beneficial bacterial absorb many carcinogenic substances, rendering them inactive. In an unhealthy gut, toxins do not get mopped up and are more likely to make it into the bloodstream, especially if the gut leaks, causing increased toxicity in the blood and brain. Increased toxicity in the brain is speculated to be one of the culprits of autism, dyslexia, schizophrenia, ADHD, and depression.

When the gut flora gets out of whack, openings abound for opportunistic bacteria. Not only is the gut's protective bacterial lining lost, but some bacteria can breach the gut, opening it up to increased permeability. Due to their spiral shape, bacteria like *Spirochaetaceae* and *Spirillaceae* have the ability to push apart intestinal cells, compromising the integrity of the intestinal walls and allowing substances through that would not normally get through. Another culprit is *Candida*, a type of fungus usually kept in check by a healthy microbial ecosystem. When *Candida* has the opportunity to thrive as a result of antibiotics or a carbohydrate-based diet, it takes over. It transforms from a harmless one-cell state into an active state, growing long, stringy filaments called *hyphae* and putting "rods" through tissues of the body. This process begins in the gut and then spreads to other organs. When the gut barriers are breached, a river of toxicity flows from the gut through the body and ultimately into the brain.

# WHAT TO DO IF YOU HAVE TO TAKE ANTIBIOTICS

Antibiotics are an important tool in our arsenal of health. Today, however, prescriptions for these life-saving drugs are too often overused. Doctors pass out antibiotics at the slightest provocation instead of waiting to see whether symptoms resolve on their own. These microbe-killing drugs not only kill the bad guys, they also leave a wake of good-bug destruction, drastically affecting the ecology of microbes on and in the body. One round of antibiotics has a profound influence on the gut flora; after two years, the diversity of the population still does not equal that which existed before treatment. If antibiotics are absolutely necessary, here are some guidelines to support a healthy ecosystem during and after treatment:

- **Request a prescription for Nystatin.** In the early days of antibiotics, doctors noticed outbreaks of *Candida* after antibiotics were taken. Nystatin, an antifungal medication, was commonly prescribed along with broad-spectrum antibiotics to combat the overgrowth. However, this practice has fallen out of medical fashion. You can also take antifungal herbs that do not require a prescription, but it's important to work with a practitioner to help guide the process. If you have to kill the bad guys, keep your *Candida* in check.

- **Take probiotics during antibiotic treatment**. A course of antibiotics kills bad bugs and good bugs indiscriminately, causing diarrhea, gas, and bloating and in some cases leading to *C. diff* infections. To mitigate antibiotic-associated diarrhea (AAD), supplement with Lactobacillus GG (found in the supplement Culturelle) or VSL#3 (a probiotic supplement with a number of strains). For those who suffer from recurring *C. diff* infections, *Saccharomyces boulardii* (available as a Florastor brand supplement) can help prevent future infections and AAD. Check your local pharmacy or purchase products online.

- **Avoid natural sugars,** including honey and fruit. *Candida,* other yeasts, fungi, and bad bacteria flourish on sugar and processed carbohydrates. Unfortunately, these foods dominate our Western diet. During a course of antibiotics and for two weeks afterward, try to keep dietary sugars low. Doing so prevents the growth of opportunistic microbes that seek to fill microbial niches they shouldn't.

- **Take all of your antibiotics.** Once you're feeling better and your symptoms are desisting, it is easy to stop taking antibiotics, as the job appears to be done. However, antibiotic treatments need to be seen through to the last pill. When you don't finish a treatment, you kill weak microbes and leave the stronger ones behind, creating an environment in which antibiotic-resistant microbes thrive. The result: drug-resistant pathogens are more likely to cause harm in the future. You don't want to create super bugs. Finish what you started.

- **Take probiotics and prebiotics after treatment.** After the microbe apocalypse has come to an end, continue to give your microbe populations the building blocks they need in the form of prebiotics. These foods (onions, leeks, garlic, Jerusalem artichokes, asparagus, and bananas) stimulate the growth of bacteria in the digestive system. In addition, take probiotics to add diversity to a population that needs to rebuild itself.

- **Eat homemade fermented foods,** including vegetables (see page 221) and kefir (see page 222). Consume a small portion at every meal for at least two weeks.

# TWEAKING THE ECOSYSTEM:

## PREBIOTICS AND PROBIOTICS

When minor tweaks are needed in your microbial ecosystem, there are two things that can bolster gut health: prebiotics and probiotics. Each plays a critical role in stimulating a well-functioning gut.

Prebiotics are nondigestible, nonliving foods and nutrients that feed bacteria. Similar to insoluble fiber, prebiotics pass through the system adding little nutritional value. However, they selectively stimulate growth and activity in the intestinal microflora. In a sense, they are the foods and nutrients that our good bacteria need to thrive and survive.

If you want a healthy population of the good guys, it is imperative to feed them lots of prebiotics. Vegetables and fruits are full of natural prebiotics. However, sometimes your good guys need a boost, such as during a course of antibiotics. For these times, there are prebiotic supplements, which can help prepare your gut for repopulation after antibiotic use.

The other way to tweak your microbial ecosystem is to introduce new microbes into your gut through probiotics. Probiotics are one-celled microorganisms (often bacterial) that are believed to help populate the gut with good bacteria and add to the diversity of the gut flora population. They come from foods and are found in supplement form.

Historically, many cultures have consumed probiotics in the form of fermented foods—from kimchi in Korea to sauerkraut in Europe to poi in the Pacific Islands. Fermentation was a natural preservation method for most of human history. In addition to adding "shelf life" to dairy, vegetables, and other staples, it was a valuable way to expose the digestive system to helpful bacteria. Once staples in people's diets, fermented foods are rich with protein, vitamins, minerals, and healthy bacteria that bolster gut flora. Fermentation also increases the bioavailability of nutrients in some foods. With the advent of modern preservation techniques, however, fermented foods have lost their prominence in the Western diet, and our guts have suffered.

Probiotic foods have become trendy in recent years. Probiotic yogurts, for example, fill grocery store shelves. Buyer beware when purchasing probiotic pills, fortified yogurts, or kombucha (a fermented tea beverage). Probiotic foods should call out the strains they contain on the label; expect to see five or more specific strains of bacteria. If the strains are not explicitly called out, don't buy into the marketing. Also, microbes have specific jobs. When you have a problem, you need to find the best microbe for the job and avoid feeding the bad guys.

## TIPS FOR MAINTAINING GOOD GUT FLORA

- **Avoid antibiotics if you can.** Antibiotics kill the bad guys, but they also kill the good ones. It can take years for your gut flora to recover from the microbe-killing carpet bomb. Before you pop pills, make sure that you need them. If you don't have another choice, practice damage control by following a gut-healing protocol during and after your course of treatment (see Chapter 8: Troubleshooting Your Gut).

- **Eat a real-food diet.** Diets high in carbohydrates, sugars, and refined foods limit the diversity of your gut flora and feed bad gut-riders like *Candida*. You want a healthy population working for your gut.

- **Eat fermented foods.** Fermented foods, including sauerkraut and yogurt, are full of beneficial microorganisms. It's best to make your own to maximize freshness and get the best cultures—see page 221.

- **Don't stress.** Good bugs like the good life. They don't like stress and will not stick around if you are sending signals that you are in distress.

# A NEW ART: UNDERSTANDING THE MICROBIOME

Only for the last hundred years have we known about the bacteria living on us and in us. The understanding of the microbiome is a rapidly changing science.

In the recent past, most of our information about the body's passengers came from cultures grown on Petri dishes. However, 85 percent of bacteria don't culture because they are anaerobic, meaning that they live without air. Technological limitations restricted our views of what happens inside us. Only since the advent of genetic sequencing and plummeting sequencing costs have our views begun to expand and reshape our picture of the microbiome and its anaerobic diversity.

The scientific community is pushing to attain as much information as possible. Data is being gathered and compiled. Citizen science groups like uBiome and American Gut (part of the Human Food Project) are helping to collect wider samples. But again, the science is new and changing fast.

As we begin to see the differences among individuals' gut biomes both within and between cultures, one important question arises: how can we manipulate the microbial population in the gut? Many issues are brought up, such as:

- Can strains of bacteria created in commercial operations be successfully transferred to the gut?
- Does ingesting strains of bacteria affect the gut population and ecosystem?
- Does home fermentation guarantee that we feed our guts the good guys without adding more unknowns and bad bugs?

It's a wild new world. And we can only move forward with open and curious minds seeking to understand this universe within.

## WHAT YOU CAN DO ABOUT INFLAMMATION FOR OPTIMAL HEALTH

**Eliminate from your daily diet foods that fight back,** including grains, legumes, and, most important, wheat and its component gluten. Make sure to check labels. Just like sugar, gluten is sneaky and makes its way into many packaged foods!

**When you cheat, cheat the smart way.** Avoid wheat altogether and instead cheat with less aggressive grains, such as corn and rice.

**Bolster your micobiome.** Eating a diet rich in nature's foods will bolster the good microbes and keep the bad ones in check.

**Take measures to support good gut flora,** especially if you must take antibiotics. Take pre- and probiotics. Consider a restorative diet to nourish and reboot a healthy gut (see page 216).

**Be an educated health-care consumer.** Stay informed. The science of chronic inflammation is not given its due.

**Address health problems by making better food choices.** Don't jump straight to treating symptoms; treat the underlying problem first.

**Chapter 5**

# ACTIVITY: MOVING AND FUELING FOR MAXIMIZED BENEFIT

## Personalizing activity levels for optimized health

## MOVE, MOVE, MOVE

To achieve optimal health, you must do what your body is designed to do. This means moving as well as eating what you are supposed to eat. Our primal forefathers had to earn what they ate. Natural periods of activity (searching for food and running from predators) and rest were built into daily life. In today's affluent societies, physical activity must be sought out. If you want to be healthy, you have to choose to move.

Exercise does wonders for your body. Your heart is strengthened when you make it work hard. A stronger heart is more efficient, even when resting. When you challenge your muscles, they get stronger and more toned. Your bones become denser and more resilient when you lift weights, preventing osteoporosis down the road. Some experts say that exercise even boosts cognition and makes you smarter.

Additionally, exercise changes the way nutrients are partitioned on a cellular level. When you exercise, your cells get better at dealing with insulin. Exercise is an important tool in combating glucose issues and, in some cases, can even help reverse the effects of type 2 diabetes. The need for activity—from standing at your desk to taking short walks to lifting weights—is an important part of your genetic makeup.

# STRATEGIES FOR INCREASING ACTIVITY

Being active is a way of life, not something you check off the to-do list every day. Adding activity need not be a daunting task. With a little forethought, increasing movement can be a pleasurable addition to life as well as a tool for making you healthier. Here are a few ways to get into the swing of things.

**Set realistic goals.** Adding activity can be as simple as increasing how much you move or walk every day. If exercise has not been a part of your routine, start small. Choosing goals that are attainable will give you early success and help you avoid the painful side effects of exercising too hard. Build up your strength and tolerance gradually.

**Walk more.** Cars are convenient. It is easy to forget that you can easily walk to accomplish some of your errands. Put your car in park and try doing some of your errands on foot or bike. Enjoy the journey, not just the destination. Walking will do as much for your happiness as it does for your health.

**Make activity fun.** When you enjoy what you do, you are likely to do it more often. Choose activities that are enjoyable to you. Whatever it is—jumping on a trampoline, hiking in the woods, or playing kickball—fun exercise can help make activity seem like a break rather than a chore.

**Seek community.** Working out with others can provide extra encouragement, accountability, and motivation to push further. Find others who share the same goals and set regular times to get together for your chosen activity.

**Don't compare yourself to your glory days.** It is easy to compare yourself to the person you were years ago, when you played sports in high school or were in tip-top shape. Don't hold yourself to the same standards you held when you were eighteen. Your body changes, and so should your expectations.

# CHOOSING THE RIGHT
# ACTIVITY FOR YOUR BIOLOGY

The health benefits of activity are undeniable. Just as your body functions best with certain foods, it also functions best when you are active. But you need to make sure the exercise you choose provides the right types of stressors. Some stressors stimulate the body to become stronger, while others weaken the body. For most people, moderate activity is enough to achieve optimal health without overtaxing the body.

Extreme athletes, who constantly push themselves to their limits, need to be careful about getting the proper rest. For hunter-gatherers, work and rest came in cycles. Winter forced our early ancestors to slow down. Hunting large game allowed them to rest between meals so they were not working hard every day. Though demanding, life was not always strenuous from morning to night.

Today we live in an athletics-obsessed culture. Extreme sports, endurance training, and one-upmanship in physical feats are the norm. To hear a coworker talk about his weekend marathon or triathlon on a Monday morning is not uncommon. This is a recent phenomenon. Ask your parents what they did with their spare time when they were younger. They probably weren't working out at the gym!

In the 1960s, heavy physical activity was thought to be bad for you. But as an article in the *New York Times* reported, by the 1970s this view had lost popularity in favor of the "new conventional wisdom—that strenuous exercise is good for you." This was followed in the 1980s by the rise of running and the introduction of new types of aerobics. Cities and small towns alike built exercise stations on public trails, broadcasting the message that working out is important to health.

Do not let exercise trends get in the way of what is healthy for your body. Extreme fitness (ultramarathons, Ironman triathlons, and so on) can be fun, but you need to make sure your exercise provides good stressors that make you stronger, rather than weaker, by avoiding adrenal fatigue and excess inflammation. Sometimes this means backing off for a time and choosing activities that are less stressful.

# THE DANGERS OF EXERCISE:
# GETTING FAT WHILE GETTING FIT

The Ironman Triathlon consists of a 2.4-mile swim followed by a 112-mile bike ride and capped off with a 26.2-mile run. Completing an Ironman without training is not possible. Ironman athletes train hard for two to four hours a day, burning a huge amount of calories. Even with all the extra training, though, many chunky people appear at the starting line, and even some who are fat. These demanding sports do, of course, produce plenty of svelte bodies and opportunities for some to show off their six-packs. But even in elite athletic circles, the bodies on the cover of *Men's Fitness* are the exception rather than the rule. So what gives?

Most endurance sports are fueled by carbs, and lots of them. Check out a pit stop at any marathon, and you will see sports gels, Gatorade, bananas, and other carb-tastic goodies that would send any four-year-old into a covetous tantrum. These "foods" are effective at delivering sugar to cells, which is why they fuel elite athletes. But their kick comes at a cost. Even during a period of strenuous training, increased carbs have the same results for super-athletes as they do for the rest of us: carbs affect insulin levels, encourage fat storage, spark inflammation, and impair immune function.

If even elite athletes who work out prodigiously can be fat, those of us who are ordinary gym-goers should take note. No amount of exercise is going to give you carte blanche to eat whatever you want. Fueling smartly is imperative, especially when your appetite is increased from exercise. You don't want to get (and/or stay) fat while you are getting fit.

Someone who is lean and doesn't exhibit metabolic derangement can eat dense carbs like sweet potatoes post-workout. For someone who has to lose fifty pounds, however, it would be better to keep carb intake low until insulin sensitivity is regained. See how to test your insulin sensitivity on page 126.

# FOR ATHLETES: SMART TIMING OF CARBS TO AUGMENT PERFORMANCE

Most casual gym-goers do just fine with smart fueling with nature's foods and carb monitoring. Intense activity for athletes, however, demands nuanced fueling for performance and recovery. Physical activity demands more energy from your cells. You can use your hungry cells to your advantage. Eating quality carbohydrates can be a great tool for attaining your athletic goals, whether you want to fill the tank without getting a spike of insulin, demand more performance from your body, or fuel smartly during extended physical activity.

## EAT GOOD CARBS PRE-WORKOUT TO ACHIEVE BETTER PERFORMANCE

Priming the pump with a bit of pregame fuel can be the difference between a personal record and a workout that's only so-so. The extra glycogen (glucose) coursing through your arteries just might give you that little extra bit of performance that you have been chasing. Lighter foods in small quantities will do the trick, like a portion of baked sweet potato.

Again, know your body. Some people feel nauseated if there is food in their stomachs during a workout. For others, small amounts of carbs are just the thing to get them going.

## SMART FUELING DURING EXTENDED WORKOUTS

You need fuel or your body stops. Your body naturally has enough energy stored in the muscles and liver to sustain a certain amount of activity. Once you've exhausted your stored energy, continuing exercise hurts unless you refill the tank. For extended activity, a steady refuel supply is essential to keep going and going and going.

To refuel on-the-go, most athletes reach for a shiny silver pouch of liquid fuel. Don't be fooled. These little space-age wonders are full of funky ingredients. If you plan ahead, you can make your own sports gels that are in line with your nutritional values.

A side note: Some people prefer less sugar during extended periods of exercise. Play around with a variety of flavors for exercise fuel. When you turn your back on packaged "performance" foods, you might find that you can better give your body what it needs—especially if that is more salt and less sugar.

> **Don't be fooled by shiny silver pouches of liquid fuel. Their kick comes at a cost.**

## POST-WORKOUT FUELING: HOW TO EAT CARBS WITHOUT SPIKING INSULIN

Incorporating carbs the right way can help you get needed energy to your muscles without the negative effects of insulin. One of the best times to incorporate carbs into your diet is post-workout. When you move hard, your body uses the energy stored in your liver and muscle cells. When you are done, your cells are left starving and screaming for nutrients. You want to take advantage of your cells' hunger window and deliver the protein and carbs they crave to refill depleted stores. If you do so soon enough after exercise, you won't get a hit from insulin. Score!

Some say that the optimal time for this carb- and protein-rich refuel is less than fifteen minutes after a workout. Thirty minutes out is still a good time, but the clock is ticking. After an hour, your body will be back to its baseline for responding to elevated glucose in your blood.

Plan ahead if you want to take advantage of this window of opportunity. Your post-workout fuel needs to be handy right when you finish your last rep. This snack should include carbs to feed cells and protein to repair

**Take advantage of cells' hunger window after workouts so you can shuttle glucose into cells without a hit of insulin.**

them. Stretching, debriefing a workout with your friends, or driving home does not count as workout time. Be smart: have what you need on hand to refuel so you don't have to rush or skip other important post-workout measures, such as mobility training and stretching.

## CARBS POST-WORKOUT: NOT FOR EVERYBODY

Store shelves offer a growing range of post-workout products promising improvements in body composition and gains in performance. However, casual gym-goers and athletes need to be wary of these claims. Filled with carbs, these products (such as sports drinks and recovery shakes) are not for everyone.

Those who are overweight should avoid flooding their bodies with extra carbs. Excess body fat is a sign that insulin is not doing its job. If you fall into this category, give your cells a break to get your body on track. Consume only 20–40 grams of protein post-workout. Once you have leaned out, you can add carbs.

## QUICK TIPS FOR ATHLETES ABOUT CARB INTAKE

Balancing carbs and endurance can be a tricky tightrope. Here are a few rules to keep you on the right track.

**Be picky about your carb sources.** Wonder products may leave you feeling like you just strapped on rocket boosters to fly to the moon, but nature makes the best fuel. Stick to complex carbs from real foods so you don't burn up shortly after liftoff.

**Stay away from fructose.** Due to its high sweetness level, a lot of sports products use this sugar to keep calories low. But you want your sugars to go straight to your muscles, not to your liver.

**Know what you need.** When you are adding extra carbohydrates to fuel extended activity, know your tolerance. The goal is to refill the tanks without going overboard and triggering insulin responses and fat-storage mechanisms. Track yourself. Monitor how you feel. Use trial and error to tweak your plan for optimized performance.

**Be honest about your goals.** Reasons for engaging in endurance-type sports or training abound. For some people, it's just fun. For others, it's a way to manage stress at home or at work by making the body simulate that running-from-lions feeling. For many people, weight loss is the goal. If you are in this last group, be smart and diligent. No amount of working out is going to give you a free pass to eat what you want. Even with intense training, diet needs to be the foundation of a healthy lifestyle. If you aren't getting good nutrition, no amount of running is going to shed those extra pounds.

**Make your own fuel.** Make your own gels and recovery formulas. Sports supplements are expensive in terms of cost and health. Formulating your own fuels, tailored to your activity, is easy and will result in a better-quality product. Again, know yourself. If you are metabolically compromised (overweight or experiencing insulin insensitivity), simple carbs can spike insulin, especially in fast-delivery liquid or gel forms.

## ACTIVITIES
## YOU CAN DO FOR OPTIMAL HEALTH

**Infuse your lifestyle with easy movement,** like walking, hiking, or throwing a Frisbee around. Make it a shared activity with your friends.

For more intensive activity, **choose exercise that is right for your body,** reducing stress instead of causing it. Listen to your body. Take a rest if your routine is doing you more harm than good.

**Fuel smart.** Don't fuel hungry muscle cells with empty carbs or fructose bombs. Choose proteins and complex carbs that won't spike your insulin.

**Experiment with the timing of your activity fuel** to increase performance and health. Do your carb and protein refuel within thirty minutes after a workout.

**Don't be swayed by products marketed to athletes,** which are full of sugar. Instead, make nature's power foods your smart sources of energy.

# PART III

## YOUR BODY, YOUR RULES

An optimal health cookbook

## Chapter 6

# A STEP-BY-STEP GUIDE TO SELF-MONITORING

**Tests, tools, and tricks to help you lose weight, detect hidden inflammation, manage stress, and optimize performance**

## THE IMPORTANCE OF MAKING YOUR OWN RULES

Want to make changes in your weight, but trendy diets have failed you? Want to be proactive in keeping your good health? Exercising but not seeing progress? Eating right but not seeing results? Want to head off or reverse disease and illness? While general guidelines set you on the road to the finish line, they sometimes fall short of taking you all the way.

Each of us has a unique biology. Our tolerances for foods, stress, and activity vary. We are in different stages of life. General guidelines don't factor in your specific makeup or environment. Your body is a dynamic biological system that is constantly changing. What you did three years ago is not what you should be doing now. You need to adapt to see continued results.

At the same time, the health world is complex. General guidelines don't always address specific needs. The health-care system can be sick-care, not well-care. The sick often get the most attention with their immediate problems. Those who want to be proactive about their health may not receive the desired attention.

Armed with science and a few tools, you can become more knowledgeable about your own health. With a commitment to listen to and observe your body and act on your findings, you can develop guidelines that work specifically for you. You can also track health markers in order to address and treat warning signs before they become problems. How? By building self-knowledge through monitoring and experimentation.

Self-monitoring and experimentation are valuable ways to gain a better understanding of your body and create guidelines that work for you. While the effort involved may seem daunting, if you choose to engage you will enter into a fascinating realm of self-discovery. You will understand your body and learn to serve it better. This approach can help answer questions such as:

- How do I lose weight?

- How can I better listen to the messages my body sends?

- Why do I still carry fat if I am diligent about my diet?

- Which foods are most likely to make me fat?

- What markers can I look for before I get sick?

- How are my cells responding to insulin?

- How can I tell if I have hidden inflammation in my body?

- How do I know whether the exercise I am doing is causing more harm than good?

## WE ARE ALL EXPERIMENTERS

Whether we realize it or not, we have all participated in self-experiments. When you eat a new food or try a new activity, you are experimenting. If you enjoy what you eat, you will eat it again. Conversely, if you have negative reactions or don't enjoy the food, you will choose to pass the next time. In either case, you do something and observe the outcome. You modify your behaviors now that you are better informed.

This chapter helps you approach your health in new ways by providing you with tools for obtaining optimal health and tracking how far you have to go to reach it. Experiments range from simple observations that require nothing more than counting to tests that require a doctor's order and lab expenses.

Don't be intimidated. You don't need every test. And you don't need to track for a long time. Monitoring is not managing an illness (sick-care). You use monitoring to optimize wellness (well-care). Think of it as an adventure for optimal health. Pick and choose what is most relevant or interesting and dive in. The results can be enlightening and life-changing.

## SETTING UP EXPERIMENTS

If you are seeking insights about your body, self-monitoring and experimentation can be revealing. It's not hard. A little planning and foresight is all that is necessary. Here are some simple tips:

- Set up experiments ahead of time. Be specific about what you are trying to learn.

- Limit testing to one or two variables at a time. For example, perform the test at the same time of day, under the same stress levels, or with the same foods.

- Be curious. Look for anomalies in your data. Ask yourself what the causes could be. Develop and test your hypotheses.

- Before you draw conclusions, be critical of your data. Ask yourself if other factors could have influenced what you observed.

- Be clear about your assumptions. Does your data support or reject your underlying assumptions? If your data does not support your assumptions, how could your assumptions be wrong?

- Good science is repeatable. Try your experiment again.

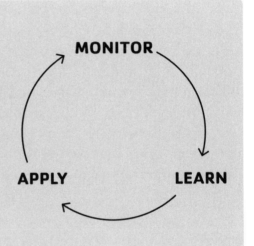

In the context of well-care, monitoring is a tool to learn more about your body and collect insights that can be applied to improve your life and health. What you monitor changes. The goal is to grow in your knowledge about yourself.

## A WORD ABOUT "NORMAL"

In this section, you will see the words "in range," meaning that your numbers look good, and "out of range," meaning that your numbers could use some improvement. The values and ranges you see will not always correspond with standard ranges. This raises the question, what does "normal" mean? Truth be told, normal is arbitrary, and it changes.

Let's take blood pressure, for example. Forty years ago, medical schools taught that 100 plus your age was normal; normal blood pressure for a sixty-five-year-old would be 165. Today your blood pressure has to be under 120 or you are in heart attack territory and need drugs fast! Cholesterol measures have changed too. As recently as 1962, *Current Diagnosis and Treatment*, a reference book for doctors, stated that normal total cholesterol ranges from 150 to 280 mg/L. Doctors today say that values should be under 200 mg/L.

While our standards have changed, clinical outcomes have not necessarily improved. Blood pressure and cholesterol metrics are the two most commonly cited indicators for heart attacks. More people monitor and treat them than ever before. However, 50 percent of heart attack patients have "normal" cholesterol and blood pressure. Normal is not the sole predictor of future health.

To further confound the issue, most guidelines are based on the averages from a diverse population. As we know, the average population in a country like the United States is not the ideal specimen of health. Aspiring to be "of average health" is like aiming for a C in a class that grades on a curve. Instead, you should aspire to be in tip-top shape for optimal energy, performance, and long-term health. You don't just want to find out that you already have a problem; you want to see red flags early and avoid problems altogether.

As a result, the numbers given here as "normal" are based on optimal health and longevity. While some doctors will look at your numbers and say that you are fine, you

> You don't want to find out that you already have a problem; you want to see red flags early and avoid problems altogether.

now have the tools to raise red flags for yourself. No one cares about your health more than you do.

# QUICK GUIDE FOR EXPERIMENTS

Here is a list of tests to run to help work toward specific goals—from losing weight to optimizing performance.

## To lose weight

BEGINNER Count carbs (see page 105) and try to stay within a healthy range.

INTERMEDIATE Monitor baseline blood glucose levels with a glucometer (see page 119).

ADVANCED Use frequent glucose testing to determine your responses to meals, stress, and other variables (see page 123).

## To test the effectiveness of a new diet

BEGINNER Track weight when changing your diet with tools such as the Withings scale (see page 115).

INTERMEDIATE Compare blood work before and after a diet change (C-reactive protein test to check inflammation levels, cholesterol panel, HbA1c—see pages 166, 153, and 130, respectively).

ADVANCED Monitor blood glucose continually with a Dexcom monitor (see page 133).

## To decrease inflammation

BEGINNER Count carbs. Avoid inflammation-causing carbs (wheat, corn, and rice) and eat more anti-inflammatory foods.

INTERMEDIATE Test inflammation levels with a C-reactive protein test and avoid exercises that overly tax muscles.

ADVANCED Determine food intolerances through food elimination tests (see page 168).

### To optimize performance

BEGINNER Use basic indicators of look, feel, and performance to tinker with optimal carb levels.

INTERMEDIATE Monitor cortisol response to activities through adrenal stress index testing (see page 180), and plan more strategic exercise breaks before your body starts to wear out.

ADVANCED Determine optimal workout and diet cycling based on specific performance goals.

# WORKING WITH YOUR DOCTOR

Some tests in this section require a doctor's order. Find a doctor who can help you gain the knowledge you need and interpret the results. A supportive doctor can be a valuable ally. Keep these ideas in mind when working with your doctor:

**Ask for what you need.** No one cares more about your health than you do. Speak up for what you want.

**Make a list of what you want and why**. Have a clear, written list of the tests you want performed. Have a succinct reason for each test in case a question comes up.

**Ask ahead what insurance will cover.** Know your insurance company's reimbursement rules. Often more tests will be covered than you think. Many plans include routine blood work at least once a year.

**Be prepared to pay cash for tests.** If insurance does not cover what you are asking for, or if you want the results to be off-the-record, don't be afraid to pay out-of-pocket.

**Request pricing and shop around.** Before you get pricked, shop around for the best price. Costs vary greatly between doctors' offices, walk-in lab facilities, and online providers, and between standard cost, cash cost, and insurance cost.

**Explore online options.** Some tests don't require blood to be drawn. Test kits can be sent by mail, saving you a considerable amount of money. Tests requiring a blood draw can be run at a lab facility with a trained phlebotomist. Look online at LabCorp (www.labcorp.com) or Quest Diagnostics (www.questdiagnostics.com). Call ahead to find out if you need a doctor's prescription for a test.

**Don't be intimidated.** Learning how to navigate the system is the hardest part. Once you set up a relationship with a doctor or lab, subsequent visits will be easier.

**Find another doctor if you don't get the service you want.** Doctors are service providers. If they are too busy to provide the service you want, find someone who will.

# CHOOSING THE RIGHT PARTNER IN HEALTH

Conflicting opinions exist in the world. Doctors are no different. One doctor with an authoritative stethoscope draped around his neck may say that lab values are fine, but he may be speaking from a perspective of diagnosing sickness, not optimizing wellness. Sick-care doctors look for results that diverge from the average and respond by prescribing medication or making a blanket nutritional recommendation. Well-care doctors approach patient care as partners in health. They take basic lab results as a starting point and consider the whole picture. While a sickness-oriented doctor might look at high cholesterol results and say that it's time to cut back on fats, a wellness-oriented doctor will look deeper at the information, noting ratios of triglycerides to HDL and partial sizes in your LDL report. She may determine that your cholesterol actually looks great.

Finding a well-care doctor is finding a partner in health. You are required to do your part and follow through. The doctor curates knowledge, insight, and interpretation. Together you work toward the goal of long-term health.

In many medical schools, only a few hours of nutritional education are provided. To receive the most up-to-date information, you need to find a doctor who reads the nutritional literature, has the patience to critique efficacy studies, and possesses the bravery to sometimes go against the grain of conventional wisdom.

Your doctor also needs to empathize with your philosophies. Finding such a doctor can be difficult. Some are more comfortable with standard approaches and rely too much on medication-based remedies, under pressure from insurance companies to go through high volumes of patients. Be stalwart in your search. Great practitioners are out there. Many doctors desire patients who are engaged with and proactive about their health.

The right doctor or health practitioner will work patiently to optimize your health, utilizing medications as a last resort instead of a first line of defense. In addition, having the right partner will set you up for a long-term relationship that will serve you well as the health data monitoring industry matures. You can collect and store more personal data today than ever before, tracking information such as heart rate, blood pressure, activity levels, sleep patterns, diet, hormone levels, and glucose levels. In the next couple of years, we will see tools that collect even more personal health data with even greater ease, perhaps in the form of little bandages worn on the skin. This information is in-

> **Well-care doctors enter into patient care as partners. They work with you to optimize your health and avoid sickness altogether.**

valuable, but it is raw and subject to interpretation. You need a doctor to help you unravel the results and understand what it all means. Finding the right doctor now will set you up for success later, as the tools get better and more ubiquitous.

## CHECKLIST FOR FINDING THE RIGHT WELL-CARE DOCTOR

The time will come when you need to call in a professional to get to the bottom of an issue. Here is a list of qualities to keep in mind:

- Thinks holistically across systems of the body and across disciplines
- Explains issues, problems, and points of interest thoroughly
- Points you to resources that further your own knowledge
- Reads primary studies and talks to you about them
- Expects you to follow recommendations
- Supports patient self-monitoring and experimentation
- Uses medication as a last resort

For those seeking a sympathetic doctor or health guide, check out the Paleo Physicians Network (paleophysiciansnetwork.com). This website is a great starting point for finding doctors who are deeply committed to prescribing good living and eating habits instead of pills.

Carbohydrates

# RECALIBRATING YOUR CARB-O-METER: COUNTING CARBS TO RESET NORMAL

Category: **Food, Hormones (insulin)**

Difficulty: **Easy**

What you need: **Access to nutrition data, recording method**

Cost: **Free**

## Why this test

Dietary carbohydrates directly influence insulin in your body. Limiting carbohydrates prevents food explosions in your system and evens out energy.

## What you can expect to learn

- Determine your general range of carbohydrate consumption.

- Learn the carbohydrate load of your favorite frequently consumed foods.

- Uncover hidden carbohydrates in your diet.

## Background

Quick, how many calories in a banana? How many carbs? Even if you knew the calorie count, chances are you missed the carbs question. Given our society's obsession with calories, it is no surprise that most people need assistance to come up with the amount of carbs in a given food.

Beyond the obvious carb culprits, secret carbs weasel their way into our diets through foods such as ketchup, salad dressing, and mayo. Most of us don't even count those as carbs. When we do keep mental tallies, we forget to include the hidden carbs in unassuming foods and beverages like coffee drinks and alcohol. Chances are your counting mechanism needs some recalibration.

Eat lots of bad carbs and look fine? Don't think you are off the hook. Just because your body does not respond to poor food choices by gaining weight does not that mean it doesn't feel the hurt. A skinny girl who eats whatever she wants may be slim and trim, but she runs a high risk of hidden consequences from bad dietary choices. If she wants to have a baby, for example, she may not get pregnant because chronically high insulin can lead to hormone imbalances that result in infertility.

Collecting data is only part of the process. Take time to learn from your observations. Each night, look at your numbers. How did you do? Any carb culprit surprises? What was your daily carb intake?

## What to do

To reset your carb-o-meter, track your food for two weeks using a computer program or app such as Tap & Track. Use one that shows more than just calories and breaks down the amounts of fats, proteins, and carbs. Tap & Track, for instance, allows you to save common meals and input data on a tablet or phone while on the go.

## Interpreting the data

Here are some helpful guidelines to interpret your carb measurements:

Danger zone: > 300 grams

Weight gain zone: 150–300 grams (U.S. recommended daily allowance)

Optimal carb intake for effortless weight maintenance: 100–150 grams

Weight loss sweet spot: 50–100 grams

Ketosis: < 50 grams (see page 156 for more on ketosis)

After two weeks of tracking and observing, you will have an intuitive sense of how many carbs you are eating and which foods are the main culprits.

After working with hundreds of clients one-on-one, Mark Sisson summarized his findings with his Carbohydrate Curve. Find out more about Mark and his practical guidelines for living a low-carb life on his blog, Mark's Daily Apple.

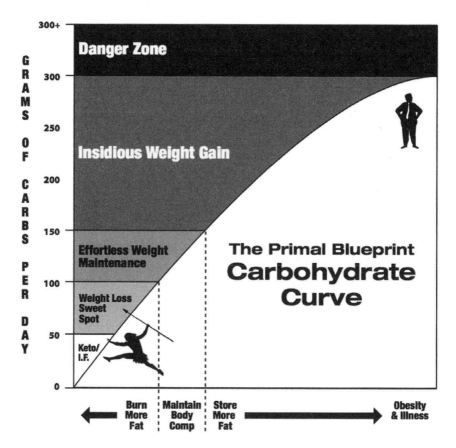

Printed with permission:
The Primal Blueprint (Primal Nutrition, 2009)

Carbohydrates

# OPTIMIZING CARBS: ASSESSING HOW YOU LOOK, FEEL, AND PERFORM TO REFINE CARB INTAKE

Category: **Food, Hormones, Activity**

Difficulty: **Intermediate**

What you need: **Self-awareness, access to nutrition data, recording method**

Cost: **Free**

## Why this test

Your body wants to run at optimal levels. This means feeling good, being alert and rested, and staying disease-free. Anything outside of optimal is a "symptom"—your body's way of trying to communicate. In order to be responsive and fix underlying causes, you have to tune in to your body's frequency.

## What you can expect to learn

- Develop carb guidelines based on your own needs, not general ranges.

- Identify the messages your body is trying to communicate through physique, performance, and feelings.

## Background

Your body tells you when you are not eating properly or taking proper care of yourself. Begin by keeping a record of how you feel throughout the day. Doing so will help you pay more attention to your body and hear what it says more clearly. Common symptoms include food cravings, energy swings, headaches, soreness, hunger, not sleeping through the night, waking up tired after a full night of sleep, pain, acne, joint stiffness, unprovoked anxiety, inattentiveness, and, for women, irregular menstruation.

Listening to your body is your best tool for optimal health. Once you start hearing the messages, you can tweak your diet to make the changes your body is asking for.

The chart opposite is an example of how you might organize your observations so that they can be helpful tools in formulating the magic numbers that work best for you and your biology.

## What to do

For a week, keep a food and symptoms log. Record as much information as you can, even if you do not think it is food related. To get started, here are some questions to ask yourself:

* How many carbs am I eating?
* What am I craving?
* When am I hungry?
* How do I feel during a workout, physically and emotionally?
* How fast can I recover from a workout?
* How does my skin look?
* What is my attention span?

> Your body is not a "set it and forget it" machine. You need to tune in to your body as it changes. The more you pay attention, the better able you'll be to interpret the messages it sends.

After you have kept your log for a week, sit down with your data and review the results. Based on the chart, what is your body trying to communicate? Are you eating too many or too few carbs?

## Interpreting the data

Deciphering the data is case specific. On the following pages are a couple of examples to illustrate how the chart can be utilized to interpret symptoms of too many or too few carbs.

### SYMPTOMS OF TOO MANY CARBS

| Look | Feel | Perform |
|---|---|---|
| Overweight | Lethargy / Afternoon energy slumps | Poor recovery and soreness post-workouts |
| Acne | Depression / Mood swings / Mental fog | Sore joints |
| Bloated | Limited attention span | Poor sleep patterns / Fatigue even after getting a full night of sleep |
| | Anxiety / Hyperactivity | |
| | Lack of focus | |
| | Sugar cravings / Midnight hunger pains / Food obsession | |

### SYMPTOMS OF TOO FEW CARBS

| Look | Feel | Perform |
|---|---|---|
| Lean or fat | Sluggish | No motivation to train |
| | Depression / Flat personality | Muscle fatigue / Slow reaction time, i.e. no snap in muscles |
| | | Slow recovery |

### INDICATORS OF RIGHT AMOUNT OF CARBS

| Look | Feel | Perform |
|---|---|---|
| Lean | High energy | Muscle energy |
| Clear skin | Consistent energy levels / Attentiveness and focus | Motivation to move and work out |
| | Mental sharpness | |

## Case Study #1

Andrew works in an office and spends most of his day sitting at a desk. Four or five times a week, he goes to the gym and runs on a treadmill after work. He runs less often when busy with his job. He considers himself a health-conscious eater.

When Andrew wakes up, he is not hungry, so he does not eat before heading out the door. On the way to the office, he picks up a cup of coffee with cream and sugar. Mid-morning he eats something quick, such as instant oatmeal or a banana. His favorite work time is the morning when his brain is sharp. By 12:30 p.m. he is ravenous. Lunch is a sandwich with chips and iced tea or a hamburger with fries. By mid-afternoon he is hungry again. He feels tired and groggy. He loses focus. He is less productive and easily distracted. To power through, he drinks a bottled Frappuccino or eats food stocked in the office kitchen—cookies, yogurt, or candy. After work he heads to the gym. Returning home, he stops for a burrito with extra veggies and black beans for dinner. Later in the evening, he might forage in the fridge for something tasty. He often eats a bowl of cereal before turning in.

He is 6'1" and 210 pounds. Even though he works out, he has a soft, round tummy. Since he works out regularly and thinks he eats healthily, the extra weight does not bother him. Andrew considers the extra pounds his natural set point.

Looking at the day, we can identify some of the symptoms Andrew is experiencing. Correlating these symptoms and numbers, we can use the chart to determine how he is doing. Andrew is eating too many carbs.

### Symptoms Log

* Does not feel hungry in the morning

* Feels hungry shortly after eating

* Has trouble concentrating in the afternoon and feels dazed

* Has extra weight around the midsection

* Carb count is 350 grams/day in sample diet

## Carb Rx

Andrew should eliminate many of the high-carb culprits from his diet by focusing on foods from nature (meats, vegetables, nuts, seeds, some starch, little fruit, no sugar) instead of processed foods. Breakfast needs to be a priority to get his day started right. He should not drink sugary beverages. With his light running on the treadmill, Andrew should eat fewer than 100 grams of carbs a day until he leans out and his symptoms improve.

## Case Study #2

Chris weighs and measures all his food and follows a strict low-carb, Paleo diet. He has a cheat meal once a week, usually on Saturday night. He is committed to CrossFit four or five times a week. He has been doing this for two years, rain or shine. In the last couple of months, he has not seen improvement in his performance, despite putting in the time. These days, dragging himself to CrossFit seems to take all the self-discipline he can muster. He feels tired and sluggish. His muscles no longer feel like they are full of energy. Chris is convinced that his cheat meals are to blame, so he cuts them out.

Chris wakes up early to make his breakfast. He has four eggs with half an avocado, sometimes adding hot salsa for flavor. Chris packs his own lunch and loves to eat chopped salads with 5–6 ounces of chicken breast. For a snack he has 27 almonds and 2–3 ounces of grass-fed beef jerky. Dinner is often a quick chicken stir-fry with onions and peppers. When he feels particularly famished, he eats almond butter straight from the jar.

Weight-conscious, Chris is lean with a solid build and 9 percent body fat. He used to be 25 pounds heavier and worked hard to shed the extra pounds. Fearing he will gain it back if he takes a break, he remains hypervigilant about his workouts and diet. Chris feels he would rather under-carb than over-carb.

Using the chart, Chris looks at his symptoms and carb numbers each day to determine how his body is responding. He needs to be flexible and listen to his body, increasing his good carbs into a more comfortable range.

## Symptoms Log

- Working out is a chore
- Muscles are sluggish
- Does not see progress in workouts
- Hypersensitive about gaining weight
- Carb count is 45 grams/day in sample diet

## Carb Rx

Although Chris's carb numbers are in the optimal range, based on the way he is feeling, he is not getting enough carbs. Even though Chris is currently lean, his history of being overweight implies that his body does not tolerate carbs well. He needs to incorporate carbs after a workout, when his body can take advantage of non-insulin-mediated glucose uptake. Eating a smart carb like a sweet potato after a workout will help him achieve increased performance without gaining weight.

# Case Study #3

Sarah is thirty-two years old and a dedicated athlete who is training twice a day for a triathlon. She wakes up early in the morning and grabs an energy bar as she is running out the door to bike before work. Sometimes during her long rides, she "hits the wall" (runs out of energy). Fearing that she is not consuming enough calories, she feeds herself on her bike ride with a packet of carb gel every thirty minutes.

Despite working out two to three hours a day, Sarah is still a bit thick in the stomach. Most people would not say she's fat, but she considers herself "skinny fat." She wishes she could cut back on calories but figures that since she is working out so much, she needs the energy. The alternative is running out of steam more often. Sarah consistently gets adult acne. While she considers herself too old for acne, she attributes it to sweat from her intense workouts.

When done with her morning workout, Sarah eats a banana and eggs before heading to work. At work she feels energized in the morning. Since she makes her own lunch, she is not tempted to go out. One day she goes out for lunch with some colleagues and has a Cobb salad. On that day her office celebrates a birthday. She indulges in a slice of cake, thinking that she's earned it and will burn off the calories later. After work she heads to the pool for a swim, fueling up with a Gatorade. Finished, she heads home for a dinner of salmon with green beans.

She refrains from dessert after dinner, but she can't stop thinking about sweets. She obsesses over cupcakes and ice cream. Most of the time she doesn't give in, but once or twice a week she does. Sarah has lots of energy but frequently feels a little down. She can't point her finger at anything that would make her feel this way. Work is going well, and she has more friends than ever from her new training. But something still feels off.

Using her daily carb number, Sarah determines that her carbs are high. Based on her activity level, though, she thinks her carb consumption is appropriate. She looks at her symptoms to determine whether this is the case.

## Symptoms Log

- Runs out of energy frequently
- Has cravings
- Feels depressed
- Has acne
- Carb count is 185 grams/day in sample diet

## Carb Rx

Sarah should clean up her carbs by eating more natural foods to fuel her activities. Processed sugars from performance products, if not tolerated well, can lead to many of the problems she is experiencing, such as acne. Adult acne is a symptom of inflammation in the body. Cleaning up the quality of carbs can also help with depression. Eating nature's foods, as we are built to do, can be one of the first lines of defense against the blues.

## TOP THREE TRACKING TOOLS THAT YOU NEED NOW

**Withings scale:** It's easy to remember your lowest or highest weight. But what happens in between? What are your body's natural rhythms and cycles over a month and over a year? The wireless Withings scale tracks your weight and will keep you honest in how you think about it. Its simple design enables you to visualize your data on your phone or computer. This is one of the best scales on the market and is a must-have tool in your arsenal of health.

**WellnessFX:** This company offers a variety of blood tests that give you access to markers that most healthy people never have the opportunity to see. Not only do you see valuable and insightful metrics, you gain one-on-one time with doctors who help you understand the data and provide proactive, actionable advice. Its intuitively designed interface allows you to track your progress over time and see the results of your efforts toward improved health. Find out more about WellnessFX on page 190.

**Glucometer:** This cheap and easy over-the-counter blood tester can provide real insight into the health of your cells and how they are keeping up with your diet. But getting the information requires you to prick your finger with a needle. Get over the ouch factor and start testing today. Read on for much more about glucose testing.

## The New Scale: Introducing the Glucometer

A glucometer is like a weight scale but better. We are all familiar with weight scales. Put on weight, and the number on the scale goes up. Lose weight, and the number goes down. Pretty simple.

Other important metrics and tools are also helpful. A 20-pound gain will not sneak up on you if you keep tabs on your weight. Similarly, if you keep an eye on your blood glucose levels, other health problems that could go unnoticed and result in chronic disease won't sneak up on you either. Your blood glucose level is important. Since glucose triggers insulin, blood glucose levels are indicators of how well your body is responding to this hormone. Are your cells still listening? Or are they tired of hearing the insulin message and starting to tune out? When you familiarize yourself with the numbers, glucose levels can also tell you how your body is responding to the food you eat, such as whether the your diet is too high in sugars and carbs. If your diet is clear of blood sugar–spiking foods, high numbers can indicate high levels of stress. Testing insulin requires a doctor's order, a skilled professional to draw blood, and some fancy equipment. In contrast, testing glucose can easily be done at home.

Today, blood glucose is tested with a glucometer, which measures glucose level in a small drop of blood. A glucometer can be purchased over the counter at a pharmacy, usually for less than fifteen dollars. It comes with lancets (small needles), test strips, and a meter for reading results.

If you feel hesitant about drawing blood, no matter how small the amount, fear not. Noninvasive glucose meters are

> If you watch the scale, a 20-pound gain will not sneak up on you. If you watch your glucometer, metabolic derangement will not sneak up on you either.

on the way. Companies like Echo Therapeutics are developing needleless glucose monitors that read glucose levels through the skin with a bandage-like patch. While these systems are out of the price range of most casual experimenters, we can look forward to lower prices and more tools using this ouch-free technology in the future.

> **Get to know your body's hidden rhythms and the language it uses to communicate.**

As with a weight scale, how often you use the glucometer depends on your goals. Testing a couple of nights in a row before bed will give you a basic understanding of how your body is processing your daily sugar intake. If you are trying to gain a deeper understanding, lose weight, or tinker with your diet, checking five times a day for two weeks can provide useful information.

As with any new skill, you will probably need to put in some time and effort before you feel confident testing and reading your glucose levels. Be patient. A single prick provides only a snapshot of data connected to a given moment in your life. It won't reveal a wealth of secrets. Over time, however, you will get to know your body's hidden rhythms and the language it uses to communicate. Your glucose level is an easy place to go to translate a piece of that message.

## How to Test Blood Glucose Using a Glucometer

1. Purchase a glucometer starter kit at any pharmacy. Kits come with a lancet (small needle) to prick the skin, test strips to read the blood, and a meter to display the results. Instructions may vary depending on the device. Familiarize yourself with the manual before proceeding.

2. Insert a test strip into the meter. When the machine is ready, it signals you to place blood on the test strip.

3. Pick an area on your fingertip that is free from calluses. Inject the lancet shallowly into your finger to produce a small drop of blood the size of a pencil tip.

4. Dab the drop of blood onto the tip of the test strip device for analysis. After 10–15 seconds, your glucose level will be displayed on the screen.

5. Record your results. (See page 120 for details on interpreting the results.)

## Helpful Tips

• Use different fingers to avoid callus buildup.

• If you don't get enough blood, try squeezing the tip of your finger before you prick yourself again.

• Sharp needles hurt less. To minimize the ouch factor, change lancets frequently.

• Never share lancets.

• Be discreet about where and when you test. You may be proud to be testing your blood glucose in order to optimize your health, but many people dislike the sight of someone drawing blood in public.

Insulin

# YOUR BODY'S RESPONSE TO DIET: END-OF-DAY GLUCOSE TESTING

Category: **Food, Hormones**

Difficulty: **Easy**

What you need: **Glucometer and test strips, recording method**

Cost: **$**

## Why this test

Since glucose triggers insulin, with a simple test you can see how well your body is responding to this hormone. Testing a few nights in a row before bed provides a basic understanding of how your body is processing your daily carbohydrates.

## What you can expect to learn

- Discover how your body is dealing with glucose at the end of the day.
- Track trends inside your body over time.
- Spot warning signs before problems arise.

## Background

A glucose reading gives you a solid understanding of how well your body is managing your dietary carbohydrates throughout the day. Some practitioners tell you that a glucose reading is best done when the stomach is empty. However, a reading taken at bedtime gives you more information about how your body is processing foods.

## What to do

1. Perform a nightly glucose test before bed for one week.

2. Record your results.

3. Repeat the week of tests every four months.

## Interpreting the data

If you weigh yourself only once, the number is meaningless. After weighing yourself regularly, however, the measure becomes more meaningful. Just like weight, you want your blood glucose numbers to be in context and revealing over time.

Some practitioners consider these ranges a helpful guide for optimal health.

**PRE-BED GLUCOSE (MG/DL)**

| < 89 | 90-99 | 100-119 | > 120 |
|:---:|:---:|:---:|:---:|
| OPTIMAL | NORMAL | SLIGHTLY HIGH | HIGH |

Consistently high glucose levels generally mean high insulin levels. Even if you feel great right now, chronic exposure to high glucose is not good for long-term health. If your glucose is high and you aren't paying attention to your diet, don't be surprised. Our bodies were not designed for this contemporary Candyland of perpetual sugar and carbs. It isn't too late to take action, however; your cells are resilient. If you make changes to your diet early enough, your body can bounce back. Keep reading. You will find some good tools to manage your diet and create a plan that works for you.

Insulin

# WHICH FOODS WILL MAKE YOU FAT: GLUCOSE TESTING RESPONSE TO FOODS

Category: **Food, Hormones**

Difficulty: **Easy**

What you need: **Glucometer and test strips, recording method**

Cost: **$**

## Why this test

Your body is unique, and so are the foods it can tolerate. While some people might do well with sweet potatoes, fruit, or sweets, others might not. It is up to you to determine which foods keep your blood sugar levels healthy. No matter what health messages are broadcast, if a food spikes your blood sugar over your target range, you should not eat it. Using your glucometer, you can determine which foods work best with your body.

## What you can expect to learn

- Identify the trouble foods to avoid.
- Develop personalized dietary guidelines.

## Background

Testing your glucose response to individual foods will help you pinpoint what to avoid. If your body responds to foods by creating a glucose spike, don't eat them. Keep the fat cells closed.

## What to do

1. Take a baseline glucose test.

2. Eat only the food you are testing.

3. Take a blood test one hour after eating.

## Interpreting the data

### GLUCOSE ONE HOUR AFTER MEAL (MG/DL)

| < 119 | 120-139 | 140-199 | > 200 |
|:---:|:---:|:---:|:---:|
| OPTIMAL | NORMAL | HIGH | VERY HIGH |

If your blood sugar surges above the healthy ranges, don't despair. Try adding some fat to slow digestion. Test again a couple of days later. If your number is still high, eliminate the offending food from your diet.

Insulin

# GET OFF THE SUGAR ROLLER COASTER: GLUCOSE TESTING THROUGHOUT THE DAY

Category: **Food, Hormones**

Difficulty: **Intermediate**

What you need: **Glucometer and test strips, recording method**

Cost: **$**

## Why this test

A glucometer gives you new eyes to peer inside your body and check out what's happening. Incorporating this simple tool into your routines can develop your understanding of how your body processes the food you eat and how well your cells respond.

## What you can expect to learn

- Discover the effects of different foods on your glucose levels.

- Manage energy more effectively throughout the day.

- Understand whether you are actually hungry.

- Identify which meals lead to high glucose and insulin spikes.

- Familiarize yourself with your personal glucose patterns.

- Reinforce good eating choices with data.

## Background

This is a more involved way of testing glucose for those who are ready to dive into the data. It is good for people who are learning to manage their glucose levels, optimizing carbohydrates during meals, choosing the right foods for their bodies, and experimenting with their bodies' tolerance for sugars. You want your glucose levels to be consistent throughout the day, providing a constant stream of energy while avoiding roller coaster–like ups and downs.

## What to do

1. Using a glucometer as described on page 117, test your blood glucose five times a day. Record all results and all foods eaten.

2. Keep up this testing regimen over a period of at least two weeks. Over this period, you will become accustomed to your patterns.

3. Perform an initial fasting blood test immediately after waking and before eating anything.

4. Do a second and third test two hours after breakfast and lunch, respectively.

5. Take a fourth reading immediately before dinner.

6. Finally, take one more reading before bed.

## Interpreting the data

Reading the results is easy. Consider your fasting blood glucose to be your baseline. Two hours after a meal, your blood sugar will be higher but should be within approximately 20 points of your baseline. Before dinner and before bed (assuming that you are going to bed several hours after eating), your blood sugar should be close to the fasting range you measured first thing in the morning.

> With data, you can begin to piece together the story your body is telling.

If you have elevated glucose levels after meals, before dinner, and at bedtime, start adjusting your diet to see how you can get your numbers in order. Your goal is to have as consistent a reading as possible. When the glucose line doesn't move more than 20 points from baseline at any given test time, you have a constant stream of energy throughout the day. You avoid the mental fogginess, post-lunch slumps, and urges to nap that plague almost all those who eat the Standard American Diet.

Sit down with your data and do some analysis. Are your numbers sky-high across the board? Think about what in your diet could be to blame. Is your diet low-carb but the glucose numbers still seem high? If so, see the section about cortisol and stress on page 56. If you are stumped, find a doctor or other practitioner who will work with you to help you understand what's going on and why.

### FASTING GLUCOSE (MG/DL)

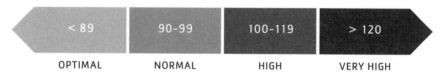

| < 89 | 90-99 | 100-119 | > 120 |
|:---:|:---:|:---:|:---:|
| OPTIMAL | NORMAL | HIGH | VERY HIGH |

### GLUCOSE ONE HOUR AFTER MEAL (MG/DL)

| < 119 | 120-139 | 140-199 | > 200 |
|:---:|:---:|:---:|:---:|
| OPTIMAL | NORMAL | HIGH | VERY HIGH |

### GLUCOSE TWO HOURS AFTER MEAL (MG/DL)

| < 99 | 100-119 | 120-139 | > 140 |
|:---:|:---:|:---:|:---:|
| OPTIMAL | NORMAL | HIGH | VERY HIGH |

### PRE-BED GLUCOSE (MG/DL)

| < 89 | 90-99 | 100-119 | > 120 |
|:---:|:---:|:---:|:---:|
| OPTIMAL | NORMAL | HIGH | VERY HIGH |

Insulin

# ARE YOUR CELLS STILL LISTENING?: GLUCOSE SENSITIVITY TEST

Category: **Food, Hormones**

Difficulty: **Intermediate**

What you need: **Glucometer and test strips, recording method**

Cost: **$**

## Why this test

You need to understand how well your cells are listening to insulin. Evidence of your cells not responding well to this hormone means that your cells are taxed and your pancreas is in overdrive. Your cells can heal, but they need time. Where you are now is a result of a lifetime of eating decisions. It will take more than two weeks of good eating to make them healthy again.

## What you can expect to learn

• Observe the health of your cells in processing glucose.

• Identify early warning signs of insulin resistance.

• Develop a baseline test and monitor over time how your cells are healing from good diet decisions.

## Background

When carbohydrates are broken down into glucose, the body uses insulin to regulate levels in the blood. With your glucometer, you can measure changes in your glucose levels and infer what kind of work your insulin is doing. With this connection in mind, it is easy to test your insulin sensitivity at home with just your glucometer and some quick (and quantified) fast-acting carbs. Potatoes and rice are good options.

Ideally, you want to perform this test every four to six months. If you have yet to rein in your carb intake and want to start changing your diet, perform this test before and after a diet overhaul. With dedication to a Paleo diet, your cells will return to normal ranges like magic. In the long term, they will thank you by giving you more energy and a trimmer body.

## What to do

Take a fasting glucose test upon waking. Eat at least 75 grams of carbohydrates. If you want to be more scientific, you can get official glucose sugar (bolus) on the Web. Test your blood glucose thirty minutes after eating. Test again one hour, two hours, and three hours after the first test.

## Interpreting the data

Baseline fasting blood glucose (mg/dL): < 89

Oral glucose tolerance test (OGTT) 1 hour after meal (mg/dL): < 140

OGTT 2 hours after meal (mg/dL): < 120

OGTT 3 hours after meal (mg/dL): back to baseline

Your glucose level should rise the first hour. At hour 1, it should be less than 140 mg/dL. At hour 3, it should have returned to near baseline fasting level. If your results are normal (your blood glucose didn't rise too high and returned to normal after hour 3), you're looking good.

If your blood glucose chart looks more like the first diagram on the following page, spiking over 140 mg/dL, you are likely to have impaired glucose tolerance and problems brewing. If your glucose level surges over 200 mg/dL, seek a doctor's help immediately. Glucose in the blood is toxic, so the higher the number, the more damage is being done to your cells. If your glucose dips below your fasting level, there is also a problem. Having blood glucose that is too low (hypoglycemia) can be dangerous. This happens when blood glucose drops below 70 mg/dL. Finally, if your blood sugar takes longer to normalize, you have just received an invitation to do more digging and take action.

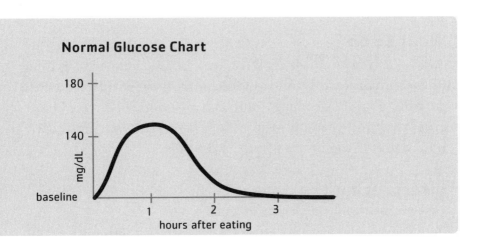

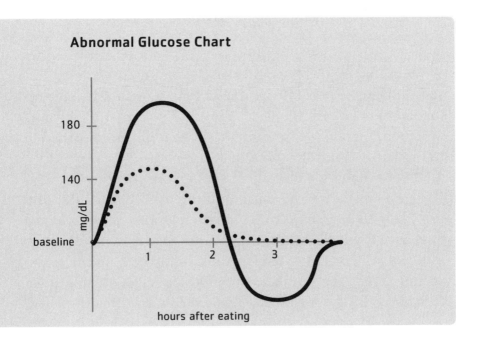

Note: If you have been following a consistent low-carb diet and are fat-adapted, your glucose tolerance test results will be skewed. To account for eating high amounts of carbs that your body is unaccustomed to, subtract 10 mg/dL from your hour 1 and hour 2 readings.

If you have impaired glucose tolerance and have yet to make dietary changes, now is the time to do so. If you are on a low-carb diet, problems with high blood sugar might be a result of beta-cell reduction, micronutrient deficiency, hormone dysregulation, or autoimmunity. It might be time to seek help to interpret results and collect more information. While you can easily test glucose with at-home tools, other factors are also at play, including insulin and cortisol. However, these inputs require professional equipment. Seek skilled practitioners to administer tests and help you interpret what's going on.

Insulin

# THE BODY'S GLUCOSE TRACKER: HBA1C

Category: **Food, Hormones**

Difficulty: **Intermediate**

What you need: **Prescription for a blood test**

Cost: **$**

## Why this test

Your glucose levels are constantly changing throughout the day. While finger-sticking is a great way to get an internal snapshot of what is happening at a given moment, it is valuable to know your body's reactions when you aren't looking. Amazingly, your body stores a record of your glucose average in the form of glycated hemoglobin, also known as HbA1c.

## What you can expect to learn

- Your blood glucose average over a three-month period
- Your body's response to changes in diet over time

## Background

It is difficult to get accurate blood averages. Blood glucose levels fluctuate from minute to minute when you are sleeping, working out, eating, or just daydreaming. One finger-stick doesn't tell the whole story. Luckily, a metric inside your blood keeps track when you are not looking—a specialized hemoglobin.

Hemoglobin is a transport mechanism inside red blood cells that carries oxygen and carbon dioxide throughout the body. Hemoglobin picks up oxygen from the lungs and travels through the bloodstream to deliver it to tissues. Once delivered, the oxygen is used to burn nutrients to provide energy to power cell activity. When oxygen is released, hemoglobin takes the by-product of the cells' work, carbon dioxide, back to the lungs to be dispensed of through respiration.

Hemoglobin can transport more than oxygen and carbon dioxide. Glucose sticks to a hemoglobin molecule to make a glycosylated hemoglobin known as HbA1c. The more glucose in the blood, the more HbA1c is formed.

In a sense, the adhesion of glucose to hemoglobin is the way hemoglobin keeps track of average glucose levels. Since red blood cells refresh every eight to twelve weeks, the amount of HbA1c indicates glucose levels over that period. The amount of HbA1c changes slowly, so it is a good test of glucose quantity.

## What to do

1. Go to your doctor and request a blood draw for HbA1c.

2. Have the test repeated every six months, or tack it on any time you get blood work done.

## Interpreting the data

Translating your HbA1c is easy. Most practitioners recommend this quick equation to convert your HbA1c to your average glucose levels:

$$28.7 \times \text{HbA1c} - 46.7 = \text{average glucose}$$

While a useful marker, HbA1c levels change with the life of cells. Folks with clean diets have healthier cells that live longer, which leads to potentially higher HbA1c levels. Those with poor diets have faster cell turnover and potentially lower HbA1c levels. Use HbA1c numbers in conjunction with the post-meal glucose test (see page 121) to get a good picture of what is happening with your blood sugar.

## HBA1C %: SLOW CELL TURNOVER (LOW CARB)

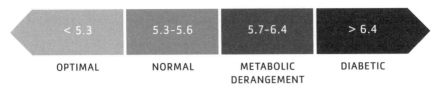

| < 5.3 | 5.3–5.6 | 5.7–6.4 | > 6.4 |
|:-----:|:-------:|:-------:|:-----:|
| OPTIMAL | NORMAL | METABOLIC DERANGEMENT | DIABETIC |

## HBA1C %: FAST CELL TURNOVER (STANDARD AMERICAN DIET)

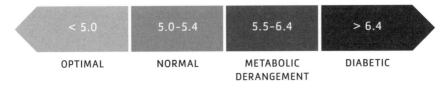

| < 5.0 | 5.0–5.4 | 5.5–6.4 | > 6.4 |
|:-----:|:-------:|:-------:|:-----:|
| OPTIMAL | NORMAL | METABOLIC DERANGEMENT | DIABETIC |

Insulin

# LEARNING FROM CONTINUAL GLUCOSE MONITORING: DEXCOM IMPLANT

Category: **Food, Hormones**

Difficulty: **Advanced**

What you need: **Prescription for the device, ability to set up your own tests and interpret results**

Cost: **$$$**

## Why this test

A continuous glucose monitor gives you a constant window into what is happening in your body. You will find that surprises abound, and your newly gained understanding will be rich.

## What you can expect to learn

- Identify unexpected culprits of blood sugar spikes.
- Compare the effects of different foods on your diet.
- Determine the best cheat meals that you can tolerate.
- See the effects of stress on your glucose levels.
- Test the effects of diet soda or other commercial food products.

## Background

For extreme self-trackers, the Dexcom glucose monitor is a tool worth mentioning. This continuous glucose monitoring system gives you the same amount of data as 288 finger-sticks a day. The Dexcom monitor is a wire inserted shallowly into your abdomen, where it remains for a week, held in place with a small patch. The patch sends a wireless signal to a handheld receiver. In addition to live glucose levels, the receiver provides easily readable trend lines that give you a window on how the data is changing in real time.

The Dexcom monitor costs a pretty penny. The base unit, which includes the device to insert the implant and the handheld receiver, currently runs $1,200. A pack of four disposable one-week patches costs $350. However, the receiver can be shared. If you have a group of friends or gym mates who are as data-conscious as you are, it is easy to divvy up the expense. Sometimes doctors and even gyms will rent out sharable units, bringing the cost of the weekly insert as low as $85. If you seek the large amount of invaluable information you get from the Dexcom, it can be well worth the price.

## What to do

1. Get a prescription for a Dexcom device.

2. Before you implant your device, set out a list of experiments and how you plan to do them (see "Interpreting the data" below).

3. Plan control studies and test runs that change one variable. Implant the device and begin your tests.

**Tip:** The Dexcom is FDA-approved to wear on the abdomen. While you cannot feel the guide wire when it is placed in fat, for those with little abdominal fat, the wire can "tickle" muscle, making it noticeable. If you have little body fat, put the device in a place that has more padding, like your tush.

## Interpreting the data

How to interpret your data depends on the tests you run. Following are samples of tests to run while wearing the DexCom implant, with some findings from my own experiences.

## The stress-glucose connection

The Dexcom monitor allows you to set alerts if your blood sugar goes above or below a designated number. I set my device to alert me if my glucose went above 120 mg/dL. Two hours after eating, my device started buzzing. I checked the reading and was astonished. The device read 180 mg/dL. How could this be? My food should not have had this effect on my blood sugar.

Two hours earlier I had eaten a breakfast of three eggs prepared with 1 tablespoon of butter from grass-fed cows—a low-glycemic meal. But my body was responding as though I had just eaten a bowl of sugary cereal. What was going on?

I was suspicious. What was the device telling me? I pricked my finger twice and did glucose tests using a hand-held glucometer to double-check. The high reading was accurate. I immediately did an audit on what I was doing and how I was feeling. I had just entered into what I considered the "zone of productivity" at work. For me, this feeling seemed positive; a little bit of adrenaline or stress made me work with extra jet fuel. I had always associated this feeling with productivity. But perhaps I had to rethink that—my body had a different interpretation. My body seemed to be reacting to this stress as a real threat.

It turns out that the stressful feeling I thought was productive was not doing my body any favors. The stress was stimulating my hormones to call for more glucose to be released into my blood. When I feel that way now, I know it is time to take a deep breath, relax, and draw my jet fuel from another source.

### Learning
Stress increases blood sugar. The solution is to take a step back and calm down.

## Cheating smart by mixing high-carb treats with protein and fat

You do your best to eat right, but at 4:00 p.m. willpower often disappears. Temptation is in your path. You can't say no. Knowing that this happens to even the most stalwart of dieters, I wanted to figure out how I could enjoy my treat while minimizing the negative effects of the extra carbs on my body.

To do this, I set up a test. The first day, I ate a milk chocolate bar by itself. This carb binge set my handheld device's warning levels buzzing. My baseline glucose level was slow to normalize after the chocolate, and for the rest of the day my blood sugar continued to roll up and down, all the while creeping up. On day 2, I ate a candy bar with two hard-boiled eggs. The results were better. The protein and fat dampened the effects of the carbs. I did not see a large spike. I repeated the process to verify my results. Eating the candy with something else minimized the ups and downs post-candy and enabled my body to recover faster. No glucose creep was seen. It was clear that eating protein and fat with a treat enabled me to avoid big upticks in blood sugar. I avoided the usual post-sugar-binge ups and downs as well.

**Learning**
Cheat smart by including some protein or fat with high-carb treats.

## Skipping meals causes glucose to soar

We get busy and skip breakfast. Sometimes I even think that I'm doing myself a favor by skipping a meal. One morning I woke up at 5:30 a.m. before leaving town for the day. My blood sugar level read 91. In my rush to get out the door, I skipped breakfast. From the moment I woke up, I was moving and busy—no time to stop to eat. At 11:30 a.m. I finally paid attention to my monitor. It read 125. For my diet, this number was high. I pricked my finger and used a test strip to make sure that the device was calibrated correctly. It was accurate. Even though I didn't eat that morning, my blood sugar was soaring. My body was treated the lack of food as a stressor and filled my blood with sugar to keep my energy up. Based on this data, skipping breakfast had the same effect as eating a Ding Dong.

Skipping meals is not always a bad thing. Intermittent fasting can be a regenerative activity for the gut and the body as a whole. However, skipping meals while continuing to run around living a stressful life is a losing combination, and it's not a good idea for those with poor blood sugar regulation. Now I take snacks on those mornings when I need to run out the door. When I do fast, I do so in a calm, collected manner that minimizes stress rather than adding to it.

### Learning
Skipping meals and being busy makes blood sugar soar.

Practice intermittent fasting during periods of minimal stress.

Prepare in advance meals that can be taken on-the-go when time is limited.

## The correlation between hunger and blood sugar level

In casual conversation, the comment "my blood sugar is low" is synonymous with "I am hungry." At times after a meal, I feel hungry within an hour. To me, it has never made much sense. If I could better understand the message my body was sending, I could better interpret what I should do about it.

During the week I spent wearing the Dexcom monitor, I decided to find out what was really going on with my hunger. I recorded each time I was hungry, and I distinguished between two different types of hunger. One was the subtle compulsion to eat that can easily be ignored. The other was an uncomfortable rumble in the belly. Each time I felt hungry, I noted in my journal the type of hunger and my blood glucose level.

Looking back at my data, these two forms of hunger were telling me two different things about my body. While the subtle compulsion to eat was associated with lower blood sugar, the uncomfortable rumble in my tummy was not. Sometimes when I was "hungry," my blood sugar was low, and I really did need to eat something to stay in range. Other times, my "hunger" was due to other factors, such as stomach emptying and contracting or a lack of satiety, and the snack that I craved was not actually needed. Even though hunger is more complex than a simple blood glucose level, it was useful to see patterns in my findings. I observed that the rumble-in-the-tummy feeling hit me consistently after I drank diet soda and ate fruit. After that, I knew that I should tune in to the subtle compulsion that indicates my body's real hunger.

### Learning

Be sensitive to different signals for hunger; the subtle voice is actually more connected to blood sugar levels.

Avoid diet soda. Even though it contains no calories, it makes the body want to eat more.

Fruit does not satisfy hunger; reach for a protein- or fat-based snack instead.

## High carbs, low willpower

This was the test I looked forward to the most. A carb binge for the sake of science—sign me up! After waking, I sat down to a breakfast of champions, which included glucose pills and a Milky Way—a total of 80 grams of carbs. I happily chomped away.

Literally two minutes later, my stomach revolted and started cramping as though it had been assaulted. I watched my blood sugar level rocket upward on my Dexcom monitor with the dreaded double-arrow warning sign. Gulp. Two hours later, my brain went fuzzy. All I wanted to do was take a nap. This feeling was familiar. Before I started eating a Paleo diet, I used to feel this way often.

This carb binge was supposed to be a momentary event. Two hours after I ate my glucose-spiking breakfast, an irresistible craving for more carbs kicked in. It felt like my body was starving and the only thing that could keep it going was sugar. I intended to get right back to eating the way I normally eat to compensate for my morning experiment, but my willpower was nonexistent. My appetite had transformed me into a monster. Normally full of willpower, I could not resist my body's urge to continue eating poorly—it felt like necessity.

Though the life-or-death cravings finally diminished by the evening, it was clear that my body still was much more sensitive to the foods I ate. My glucose levels went through big swings as I ate foods that would normally not cause such spikes.

### Learning

High sugar intake can lead to diminished willpower.

Big swings in blood sugar early in the day cause glucose creep later, even with healthy foods.

## Learnings

As I learned through experience, continuous glucose monitoring with a Dexcom can be a powerful tool to change behavior. If you would like to maximize your ability to learn about your body, the findings are worth getting a prescription from a doctor and running your own tests for a week or two. As a result of my own study, I now think twice about skipping meals. I try to address stress when it arises instead of ignoring it. I also feel confident that the Paleo diet I have chosen is the best for me and my body.

Leptin

# GAINING CONTROL OF YOUR APPETITE: TRACKING THE IMPORTANT HORMONAL MESSENGER LEPTIN

Category: **Hormones**

Difficulty: **Intermediate**

What you need: **Access to a lab for a blood draw, potentially prescription for a blood test**

Cost: **$**

## Why this test

It is easy to assume that success or failure on a diet is determined by discipline. But when your body is asking for carbs or other naughty foods, it can be persistent. Even those with ironclad willpower can't overcome a strong and loud biological drive. Cravings for carbs are a sign that the body isn't able to efficiently dip into stores of energy and fat to fuel hungry cells.

Even longtime Paleo eaters can have difficulties with cravings and transitioning into fat-burning mode. This can be a result of eating too much carbohydrate or protein, which if overeaten is processed into glucose in the body. The key to squelching cravings and succeeding on a diet is to control the hormone that leads to satiety—leptin.

Tracking leptin is an affordable metric that doesn't always require a doctor's prescription. And since leptin levels correlate with more than just appetite, you can learn a lot about your body through this single blood marker.

## What you can expect to learn

- Understand the marker involved with cravings and appetite control.

- Identify a single affordable blood metric that correlates with overall health.

## Background

The hormone leptin is the four-star general that controls appetite. You want your cells attuned to when it's time to put down the fork. But just as your cells can become desensitized to insulin, they can also get desensitized to leptin. And when cells don't hear the message, it takes more signals to get the point across. When your body continually overproduces leptin, you eat more, crave carbs, and no longer efficiently move in and out of fat-burning mode. And your tongue becomes desensitized to sweetness to boot.

When leptin is functioning properly, you are healthy, crave the right foods, properly process fat, and are sensitive to the foods you eat. Conversely, when your cells are bombarded with too much leptin, your body stores more fat and has a greater propensity for cardiovascular disease and diabetes. Your bones are also affected adversely, and you are prone to thyroid issues and autoimmune diseases. This single metric, the level of leptin, is the canary in a coal mine for a slew of other problems too.

Leptin numbers correlate closely with triglycerides. High triglycerides indicate a disruption in leptin efficiency. Some practitioners even maintain that leptin values are more telling than cholesterol. High cholesterol numbers can lead practitioners down the wrong path.

How do you control this important biomarker? Diet! What you eat changes the sensitivity of your cells. Increased sensitivity leads to more satiety. And when your leptin levels are optimal, you can efficiently burn the fat and glucose produced by the liver. When your fat metabolism functions properly, your appetite and cravings are controlled.

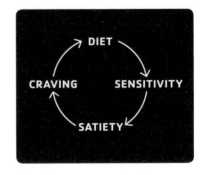

## What to do

1. Call to determine if your lab requires a prescription to test leptin levels; many do not. If possible, have the test done at a LabCorp facility, as it likely uses the preferred method of testing—radio-immunoassay (RIA). Avoid labs that test via chemoluminescence, which is less accurate.

2. Take the test first thing in the morning while fasting. Compare your values to the results below.

3. If your results are borderline or in the bad range, change your diet by reducing carbs, eating appropriate amounts of protein (no more than 1 gram for every 2.2 pounds of lean body mass), and eating more fat.

4. The test can be redone every two weeks until your level reaches the optimal or good ranges.

## Interpreting the data

Use the chart below to evaluate your test results. Women's ranges are higher than men's as a result of their increased fat tissue.

**LEPTIN: MEN**

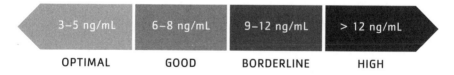

| OPTIMAL | GOOD | BORDERLINE | HIGH |
|---------|------|------------|------|
| 3–5 ng/mL | 6–8 ng/mL | 9–12 ng/mL | > 12 ng/mL |

**LEPTIN: WOMEN**

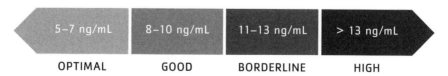

| OPTIMAL | GOOD | BORDERLINE | HIGH |
|---------|------|------------|------|
| 5–7 ng/mL | 8–10 ng/mL | 11–13 ng/mL | > 13 ng/mL |

# INTERPRETING CHOLESTEROL PANELS AND OTHER IMPORTANT BLOOD WORK

This section is a practical guide to help you better understand your cholesterol panel. You'll find helpful information, additional important tests to request from your doctor, and trends to monitor. This section provides basic information. It is not meant to provide a complete understanding of the physiology at work.

## Background

Cholesterol makes up your cell membranes and serves as a vital structural and functional component of your cells and body. In addition, it is used to create hormonal messengers. Despite its important role as a building block for cells and communications in the body, cholesterol is demonized in the public dialogue.

Both the lipid hypothesis and the diet-heart hypothesis are responsible for cholesterol's bad rap. The lipid hypothesis claims that high levels of cholesterol in the blood are associated with an increased risk of coronary heart disease. The diet-heart hypothesis says that dietary fat and cholesterol lead to increases in blood cholesterol and therefore increase heart disease risk.

At the recommendation of the National Institutes of Health, many people gravitate to a low-fat diet to avoid dietary cholesterol in an effort to be "heart healthy." At the same time, doctors run out of ink writing prescriptions for cholesterol-reducing drugs to ward off heart attacks—to the tune of $27 billion a year. The problem? Many people who have "normal" ranges of cholesterol still suffer from heart attacks every year, and many with high cholesterol do just fine. While it is true that blood lipids play a role in heart disease, the blame has been placed on the wrong culprit: fat.

Attempting to control blood lipids by reducing dietary fat has unexpected domino effects. When you eat fats, your body senses that it has enough fats for its construction needs and signals the body's material factories to take a break and use what is available from foods. As a result, the body reduces its production of fats for cell repair and growth and reconstitutes fats from food. In contrast, when you avoid fats by eating carbs, which contain virtually no natural cholesterol, your body senses a deficiency in the raw materials needed for cell growth and repair and shifts fat production into high gear.

In a world where food was scarce, the process of turning excess carbohydrates into fat (de novo lipogenesis) was advantageous. During a time of plenty, the liver would transform extra carbohydrates into triglycerides and store them as fat for later. When the time of scarcity came, the body would survive by dipping into fat stores. However, in our hypercaloric society where food is available all the time, this excess fat storage is less necessary. The result of a low-fat, highly processed diet is high triglycerides and cholesterol. And the "helpful" recommendations to avoid fats and cholesterol do more harm than good.

Unfortunately, many people take popular opinion about cholesterol as an ironclad rule. The general population might regularly check and monitor total cholesterol levels, but standard tests don't provide enough information. "Normal" ranges don't indicate optimal health, since they are an average of all patients, many of whom are already sick. As a discerning health consumer, you need to educate yourself in order to request the right add-on tests that provide the foundation for meaningful conversations with your doctor.

> **Despite cholesterol's important role as a building block for cells and communication in the body, it is demonized in the public dialogue.**

# Lipoproteins:
# The Freight Shuttle for Cell Building

Most people are familiar with the term *cholesterol*. Cholesterol is a type of lipoprotein. Think of lipoproteins as shuttles. Part protein, part lipid (fat), these shuttles allow materials from outside a cell to pass through the cell walls to the inside and deliver needed raw materials. The liver is responsible for making these shuttles. It takes spare parts and recycles materials into useful components (fatty acids, triglycerides, cholesterol, cholesteryl esters, and fat-soluble vitamins).

Once assembled, lipoproteins are sent into the bloodstream to distribute raw materials and transport important building blocks for cells. Cholesterol is used to repair and maintain cell membranes, synthesize vitamin D, manufacture bile acids and salts, and synthesize steroid hormones (progestins, glucocorticoids, mineralocorticoids, androgens, and estrogens).

When people speak of cholesterol levels, what is actually being measured is the type and quantity of lipoproteins: very low-density lipoprotein (v-LDL), low-density lipoprotein (LDL), high-density lipoprotein (HDL), and intermediate-density lipoprotein (IDL). But the term *cholesterol* is used because lipoprotein levels are indirectly measured using the cholesterol they transport.

Most doctors and insurance companies look at total cholesterol to determine if you need intervention or are a health risk. But this method is problematic. It is impossible to estimate a person's risk of developing heart disease by looking exclusively at total cholesterol. You need to understand the full picture and look at the various components. It is not about the total number but rather the quality of the cholesterol fleet. Some of the shuttles are helpful, while others are troublesome. You have to look at the specific types of vehicles (v-LDL, LDL,

> It is impossible to esti-
> mate a person's risk of
> developing heart disease
> by looking exclusively at
> total cholesterol. It is not
> about the total number but
> rather the quality of the
> cholesterol fleet.

HDL, IDL) to accurately assess what's going on. Lipoproteins can be directly measured by separating them according to density. This process, however, is far more time-consuming than the indirect measurements that are typically employed.

## HDL: The Cleaners

HDL shuttles depart from the liver on a cleanup mission and travel through the bloodstream to collect the junk that is floating around. HDL also "scrubs" arteries and veins. As it collects dangerous rogue fats, HDL brings them back to the liver for processing and recycling. Because of its benefits, lots of HDL cholesterol is desired. You should be worried if you don't have enough of these good shuttles. Ideally, HDL levels should exceed 60 mg/dL. People who exercise and eat a smart-carb diet can have lots of these good guys.

## LDL: The Distributors

While HDL cleans, LDL distributes raw materials. These lipoprotein shuttles transport needed fats, fat-soluble vitamins, cholesterol, and cholesteryl esters through the bloodstream to reach the cells. Without the needed supplies, cells can't do their jobs. Most consider LDL the "bad cholesterol"; however, LDL serves a needed distribution function. Together, HDL and LDL work to clean the blood and deliver raw materials throughout the body.

In a regular blood lipid panel, the LDL number is a crude gauge for what is actually going on. Instead of counting each individual LDL particle, labs calculate this number by using the following formula:

**LDL cholesterol = total cholesterol – HDL cholesterol – (triglycerides / 5)**

This formula was developed using certain assumptions, however: HDL must be 40 mg/dL or greater and triglycerides 100 mg/dL or lower. Calculations are thrown off when the numbers don't fit in this range, which can make the results misleading for people with metabolic syndrome, diabetes, or genetic conditions.

Not all LDL is created equal. This part of the lipoprotein fleet is differentiated yet again. Among the LDL distributors, the shuttles range in size and density. Some are large, buoyant, and fluffy (Pattern A); some are small and dense (Pattern B); and others are intermediate (Pattern A/B). A key to understanding your risk factors is to know what types and concentrations of LDL are in your blood.

Pattern A LDL moves through the blood delivering its goods. The walls of arteries are like nets, and these large, fluffy particles can't get stuck as easily as their smaller and denser counterparts. Some hypothesize that Pattern B particles are easily trapped in microscopic tears of arteries and veins. These little guys can build up, causing plaque and deposits. Gone unchecked, they may break off and float to the heart or the brain, leading to heart attacks or strokes. Others believe that large amounts of Pattern B particles indicate the presence of other problems, such as leptin resistance and downregulated thyroid function, which result in fewer cholesterol receptors. Either way, it's a smart move to avoid large numbers of Pattern B LDL.

Understanding the types of LDL particles in your system will make your cholesterol numbers more useful. Several tests can count the lipoproteins in your blood and tell you their makeup, including nuclear magnetic resonance

(NMR), lipoprotein analysis, and vertical auto profile (VAP). However, these tests are relatively new, are not part of standard panels, and may not be covered by insurance. You must request them from your doctor or naturopathic practitioner.

To dig even deeper, request an oxidized triple marker test. This innovative cardiovascular disease risk assessment test measures the number of oxidized small, dense LDL as well as oxidized Lp(a) (another risk factor for heart disease). Knowing how many of your LDL particles are oxidized gives a better assessment of your risk for hardening of the arteries (atherosclerosis).

How can you avoid the Pattern B LDL cholesterol problem? One cause of Pattern B LDL is a diet with chronically elevated carbohydrates, which leads to excess insulin. With high insulin, cholesterol production is put into overdrive through the upregulation of the enzyme that controls the rate at which cholesterol is made (HMG-CoA reductase). In addition, high amounts of trans fats (elaidic acid) and fructose activate cholesteryl ester transfer protein (CETP), contributing to small, dense LDL particles. Diets with elevated sugar, trans fats, and fructose lead to more troublemaking particles.

## Triglycerides: The Fat Makers

Triglycerides are the means by which the body stores fat. When the body has more energy (calories) than it needs, it converts the excess into triglycerides—a molecule made of three fatty acids linked to glycerol. Triglycerides are transported in the bloodstream by lipoproteins. Fat is normally stored in cells in the form of triglycerides.

Triglycerides were a vital storage adaptation when times of famine were guaranteed. Today, in our culture of abundance, it is an overused mechanism. Too many of these fat makers in the blood is a bad thing. While it is easy to assume that consuming large amounts of dietary fat results in more triglycerides, this is not the case. Unlike sugar, fat is hard to eat in excess. Fat is not addictive, it is satiating, and excess amounts are purged in the stool.

Those who eat a Paleo or low-carb diet can have triglyceride levels well below 100 mg/dL. The lower your triglycerides, the better. Low triglycerides tend to have a strong correlation with high HDL and low Pattern B LDL.

> High-carbohydrate diets and chronically elevated insulin cause high levels of bad Pattern B LDL particles, triglycerides, and low HDL.

## Trends to Watch

- Our bodies are dynamic. Cholesterol can move 20–30 points between blood draws. These fluctuations in the body are natural—no need to panic.

- Triglycerides should go down over time.

- HDL should trend up.

- You want lots of good HDL. The lower your ratio of total cholesterol to HDL, the better.

- You want your triglyceride-to-HDL ratio to be close to 1 or lower.

## Other Numbers to Monitor

When it comes to blood work, cholesterol is not the only important number you should monitor. Glucose and inflammation levels are also keys to getting a good picture of your health. When you get data on your cholesterol levels, also request your markers for glucose and inflammation. Together these markers give you a clear picture of what is happening inside your body.

## HbA1c: Your Body's Glucose Monitor

You should know your blood glucose levels, but constant monitoring isn't for everyone. Luckily, the body keeps track of your average blood glucose. Glucose sticks to a protein in red blood cells, and glucose levels are naturally tracked for about 120 days—the lifespan of those cells. With an inexpensive blood test called Hemoglobin A1c (HbA1c; see page 130), you can get a general read of what's going on with your blood glucose over a period of time. Ideal HbA1c levels are less than 5.5 percent. But like many blood tests, HbA1c is only an indicator of what is going on in your body; the results have to be interpreted correctly. For instance, if you follow a Paleo diet, cells are healthier and, as a result, have a slower turnover rate. With a longer lifetime, they collect more sugar, so HbA1c levels appear higher than they would in someone who eats the Standard American Diet. Their cells turn over much faster—in 80 days as opposed to 120—so HbA1c levels might be lower since the cells don't live as long. As with many values in medicine, context matters.

## C-Reactive Protein: The Inflammation Index

C-reactive protein is a marker for inflammation in your system. This protein binds to the surface of dead and dying cells. When the body is hard at work fighting food, injury, or infection, this marker is elevated. While C-reactive protein is an indicator that a problem exists, it does not tell you what's wrong, so it should be used only as a justification for further testing. Ideally, levels should be less than 1 mg/L. (See page 166 for more on this test.)

# Interpreting Cholesterol Panels and Other Important Blood Work

Since total cholesterol and LDL are poor indicators of health, they are not included in this chart. Instead, focus on particle size, HDL levels, triglycerides, HbA1c, and ratio of triglycerides to HDL.

## HDL CHOLESTEROL (MG/DL)

## PARTICLE SIZE (NMR)

## TRIGLYCERIDES (MG/DL)

## TRIGLYCERIDE/HDL RATIO

## HBA1C %: SLOW CELL TURNOVER (LOW-CARB DIET)

## HBA1C %: FAST CELL TURNOVER (STANDARD AMERICAN DIET)

## C-REACTIVE PROTEIN (MG/L)

Cholesterol

# HOW TO IMPROVE YOUR CHOLESTEROL IN TWO WEEKS WITHOUT DRUGS

Category: **Food**

Difficulty: **Intermediate**

What you need: **Prescription for two cholesterol panels with LDL particle size**

Cost: **$$**

## Why this test

Low-fat products have taken over supermarket shelves, yet the number of people on cholesterol-lowering medications continues to rise. Run your own test to determine how your cholesterol responds to limiting dietary carbohydrates rather than fat.

## What you can expect to learn

- Determine the effects of a low-carb diet on your cholesterol.

## Background

It is easy to conclude that eating less fat will result in lower cholesterol. But many who follow a low-fat diet don't see their cholesterol numbers drop, making it seem like drugs are the only option. Maybe it is time to test a new hypothesis: that a diet of limited and quality carbohydrates leads to healthy cholesterol levels.

## What to do

1. Assuming that you are starting with a non-Paleo diet, take a cholesterol panel that includes particle size.

2. Eliminate bad carbs: wheat, rice, oats, legumes, and fruit. Add healthy fats: avocados, olive oil, eggs, butter, nuts, and fatty meats. See below for a sample menu.

3. Record your food intake in a log. At the end of two weeks, take the same blood panel again.

4. Using the information in the "Interpreting Cholesterol Panels and Other Important Blood Work" section (see page 144), compare your results to the baseline cholesterol panel previously taken.

## Sample Menu

Get inspired by fantastic Paleo recipes online. Great resources include Balanced Bites (balancedbites.com), Nom Nom Paleo (nomnompaleo.com), and Paleo Spirit (paleospirit.com)

### Day 1

**Breakfast:** 2–3 eggs cooked in butter from grass-fed cows, ½ cup chopped frozen spinach

**Lunch:** Cobb salad with nitrate-free bacon, ham, turkey, olives, and balsamic vinaigrette

**Snack:** Celery with 2 tablespoons almond butter, 2–3 ounces Paleo Brands beef jerky from grass-fed beef

**Dinner:** 4–5 ounces steak, baked sweet potato, asparagus

### Day 2

**Breakfast:** Frittata

**Lunch:** Chicken salad

**Snack:** 2 ounces tuna with 2 tablespoons homemade mayo on cucumber slices

**Dinner:** Pork chop, steamed broccoli with butter, side salad with balsamic vinaigrette

## Day 3

**Breakfast:** 2–3 eggs cooked in butter from grass-fed cows, ½ cup grain-free granola with coconut milk

**Lunch:** Hamburger (no bun) wrapped in lettuce, grilled onions, side salad

**Snack:** Leftover frittata from Day 2 breakfast

**Dinner:** 3–4 ounces salmon, grilled squash, cauliflower rice with butter

## Day 4

**Breakfast:** 2–3 eggs cooked in butter from grass-fed cows, breakfast sausage

**Lunch:** Leftover salmon from Day 3 dinner, veggies

**Snack:** Justin's Almond Butter squeeze packet

**Dinner:** Halibut with sweet potato slices

# Interpreting the data

HDL should rise. LDL should go from Pattern B (bad guys) to Pattern A (good guys). Triglycerides should go down.

Cholesterol

# LEARNING FROM A FAT–FILLED DIET: EXPERIMENTS IN KETOSIS

Category: **Food**

Difficulty: **Advanced**

What you need: **Ketone blood tester or ketone strips**

Cost: **$$**

## Why this test

While talk abounds about the low-carb diet, the no-carb (or very-low-carb) diet is worth experimenting with. Ketosis affects dopamine receptors in the brain and is neuroprotective (protective of brain neurons). This test will give you a chance to chart your diet and its effects.

**Note:** Consult your doctor before going into ketosis. This test is not for pregnant women—stick to a smart-carb diet instead. Ketosis is not to be confused with ketoacidosis, a dangerous condition encountered by type 1 diabetics who experience uncontrolled ketone production due to lack of insulin.

## What you can expect to learn

* How your body and brain react to no carbohydrates in your diet

* The effect of high fat on basic cholesterol, particle size, and tri-glycerides

## Background

When you consume fewer carbohydrates than required for basic functioning—usually less than 50 grams per day—the body turns to other sources for energy: proteins and fats. When the body breaks down fats, by-product fuel molecules called *ketones* are created. When ketones accumulate in the blood at high levels, the body reaches a state known as *ketosis*. This state, when controlled, can offer health benefits that carb-rich diets cannot. A diet that leads to ketosis is called a *ketogenic diet*.

Ketogenic diets range from moderate to therapeutic. For example, low-carbohydrate diets include periods of ketone production and therefore are moderately ketogenic. When carbohydrate levels are severely limited, insulin production and glucose are curbed. Ketones accumulate in the blood until they become the body's main fuel source. Therapeutic levels of ketosis are used to treat many brain disorders, such as epilepsy and multiple sclerosis.

The human body was designed to function well in the presence of ketones. Ketones are used in many of the metabolic pathways where carbs exist. For many systems in the body, ketones and carbs are used interchangeably. Ketones are a preferred fuel source for the brain. This is why low-carb diets help clear mental functioning and high-carb diets leave you feeling mentally foggy. But more important, ketones protect neurons from oxidation and oxidative stress, making them less susceptible to degenerative brain diseases such as Alzheimer's. They also help regulate dopamine (the happy-maker) and have been hypothesized to help regulate depression. For decades, ketosis has been recommended by doctors as a last resort to fight persistent seizures. In addition to brain cells, other cells in the body also respond well to ketones. The ketone beta-hydroxybutyrate is a super fuel. It increases energy while decreasing oxygen consumption, making cells more efficient at doing their jobs.

There are a variety of ways to test the level of ketones in your body. The most convenient and least expensive method is to use an over-the-counter urine test that detects the presence of ketones. However, these ketone strips are not the most reliable. Ketones in your urine are being evacuated

> Ketones are a pre-ferred fuel source for the brain. This may be why low-carb diets help with clear mental function and high-carb diets leave you in a fog.

as a waste product, so they don't always correlate with the amount of ketones in your blood. And, as your body adapts to a ketogenic diet, your tissues adapt to using ketones as fuel, becoming more efficient at making and using the right amounts of ketones. As a result, excess ketones are not as present in urine, making the strips less accurate.

Testing can also be done with a ketone monitor. Monitors are more accurate but also more expensive. A ketone monitor works the same way as a glucometer, requiring a finger-prick and test strips. The amount of ketones in your blood depends on the level of ketosis your body is experiencing.

Many of the benefits of a ketogenic diet can be achieved through maintaining low to moderate levels of ketones in the blood. For those who are using ketosis as a tool to fight depression, cancer, or neurodegenerative disease, the opportunity to halt the progression of the disease or minimize the use of medication may be worth the experiment.

## What to do

To set up the experiment, identify what you are testing. Are you testing the effects of a high-fat, low-carb diet on your cholesterol? Or are you testing the effects of ketosis on your happiness? Before starting, get a blood panel taken, including LDL, HDL, triglycerides, and particle size.

Make changes to your diet. Seek the following ratio:

**1 gram combined carbohydrates and protein : 4 grams fat**

To calculate your daily macronutrient requirements, start by calculating how much protein you need, which is based on your body weight. To maintain muscle mass, you need 0.36 grams of protein per pound of body weight. The basic formula is:

**Your weight x 0.36 = grams of protein you should aim to eat each day**

For example, if you weigh 150 pounds, your protein intake should be 150 x 0.36 = 54 grams a day. If you weigh 200 pounds, aim for 72 grams of protein a day.

### KETOSIS RANGES

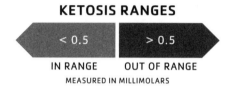

IN RANGE     OUT OF RANGE

MEASURED IN MILLIMOLARS

For many people who are already on a low-carb diet, these protein values will seem low. However, protein can also be turned into glucose. You need to be careful not to overeat this macronutrient in order to maintain the ketogenic response to fat as your primary fuel. The ideal scenario is to have just enough protein to maintain muscle, but no more. Use your ketone test monitor to follow how your body reacts to varying amounts of protein in your diet. Determine your ideal protein intake to maintain the desired level of ketosis. Tweak your diet to find your ideal measures.

A low-carbohydrate diet shifts your body (specifically your kidneys) from retaining salt to excreting it. If you find yourself thirsty or experiencing headaches, your body is suffering from mild dehydration due to this loss of salt. Supplement your ketogenic diet with salty bone broth or, if necessary, less-natural bouillon cubes to ward off side effects.

Consume 1–3 tablespoons of medium chain triglycerides (MCTs) a day, preferably in the morning to get your ketone metabolism going. MCTs are found naturally in fats like coconut oil. Isolated versions can be purchased as supplements at health food stores. Unlike other fats, MCTs burn like carbohydrates—the body utilizes them immediately. MCTs are also the most ketogenic fats, meaning that they are the most readily transformed into ketones by the body. Because they are turned into fuel so quickly, they can be used as a pick-me-up to help boost ketones in the blood when your energy is waning. A warning: MCT oil is a laxative, so build up gradually.

If you are experimenting with this diet for extended periods, connect with a doctor or dietician who can work with you. When fats are the source of 80–90 percent of your calories, specialists often recommend supplementing with a multivitamin, fish oil or cod liver oil, and selenium.

Record how you feel, what your mood is like, and what you eat. Take blood ketone tests five times a day—upon waking, two hours after meals, and before bed. When your number falls below the suggested range, cut back on proteins. After one month, take your basic blood panel again.

## Interpreting the data

Compare starting values and ending values.

How did you feel? What has happened to your weight? How did your calorie consumption change? How did your HDL, triglycerides, and LDL particles change? Did you lose weight and inches off your waistline? The case studies below are designed to give you a sense of the possibilities of a ketogenic diet.

## Case Study #1

Brian is an extreme athlete. He loves to be in the pool, on his bike, or in the gym. He regularly spends three hours a day rotating between swimming, cycling, and weight lifting. Over the years he has put his fitness to the test competing in open-water, long-distance swims; triathlons; and cycling races.

Disciplined in his training and diet, Brian was looking for a new variable to tweak in preparation for an upcoming century ride (a bicycle ride of at least 100 miles in less than 12 hours). He began to focus on increasing power output by losing weight rather than by increasing training. If he lost fat, he reasoned, his ratio of power to body weight would increase. Based on the "calories in, calories out" argument, he could either eat less or work out more. Neither was a good option to maintain his high level of performance. Instead, Brian experimented with another tool: ketosis.

Brian was diligent about recording his information. When he started, he weighed 195 pounds and had 20 percent body fat, as measured by a DEXA (bone density) scan. He took a lipid panel with particle size and a VO2 max test. He tested his blood several times a day to monitor ketone bodies and carefully adjusted his protein levels to maintain high ketogenic ranges.

Brian changed from a medium-carb, high-protein diet to a high-fat, low-carb, and moderate protein diet. He used the ketosis formula and self-testing to arrive at his ideal ratios. Here are his daily micronutrient breakdowns as a proportion of his calories:

## DAILY MACRONUTRIENT BREAKDOWN
## BEFORE AND AFTER STARTING KETOGENIC DIET

|  | Before | After |
| --- | --- | --- |
| Carbs | 35% | 4% |
| Protein | 25% | 8% |
| Fat | 40% | 90% |
| Calories | 3,500 | 4,500 |
| Activity (Hours) | 3 | 3 |

Brian's friends looked on in horror as he consumed a small bowl of olive oil and a steak with extra butter and then finished off the fat discarded from his friend's meat. But the diet did not stop there. While his fellow endurance athletes trained with sports gels, Brian packed blocks of cream cheese to chow down on long rides. When he tried to explain that he was attempting to lose weight, his friends would roll their eyes. They politely warned him about the dangers of high-fat diets and cholesterol.

Looking at Brian's numbers, conventional wisdom would dictate that over three months, his 30 percent increase in calories and 105 percent increase in fat consumption would lead to skyrocketing cholesterol, but this was far from the case.

Eating a high-fat, very-low-carb diet helped Brian lose 25 pounds from an already slim frame. Fat melted off. While his total cholesterol remained the same, a closer look shows the nuances behind the numbers. Large jumps in HDL (good cholesterol) and large buoyant particles where offset by radical declines in LDL. So, it was the good cholesterol that had changed most dramatically, not the heart-stopping small LDL particles. His aerobic efficiency also improved, while his body became less dependent on glucose. This means that his cells became more efficient at burning fat, an important advantage for long-distance athletes who require refueling.

> **Conventional wisdom would dictate that a 30 percent increase in calories and a 105 percent increase in fat consumption would lead to skyrocketing cholesterol, but this was far from the case.**

The final result was increased cell efficiency, increased good cholesterol, and less body fat. As Brian explains, ketosis was worth it, and his anaerobic activity was the only thing that suffered.

## A LOOK AT CHOLESTEROL
## BEFORE AND AFTER A KETOGENIC DIET

| | Before | After |
|---|---|---|
| Body weight (lbs) | 195 | 170 |
| Body fat (%) | 20 | 7.5 |
| Waist measurement (inches) | 35 | 31.5 |
| Food (K/Cal) | 3,500 | 4,500 |
| **CHOLESTEROL TOTAL** (standard) | 144 | 144 |
| LDL | 113 | 59 |
| HDL | 31 | 85 |
| Triglycerides | 154 | 81 |
| Triglycerides/HDL ratio | 4.97 | 0.95 |
| **INSULIN SENSITIVITY** (HOMA–IR) | 1.38 | >0.48 |
| Insulin levels before (mU/L) | 6 | >2 |
| Insulin levels 2 hours after | 36 | 16 |
| Glucose levels before (mg/dL) | 93 | 97 |
| Glucose levels 2 hours after | 108 | 83 |
| **CHOLESTEROL TOTAL** (VAP) | 141 | 145 |
| HDL total | 58 | 67 |
| HDL 2 (large, more protective) | 17 | 27 |
| HDL 3 (small, less protective) | 41 | 42 |
| **LDL TOTAL** | 61 | 77 |
| LDL 1+2 (large buoyant) | 24 | 25 |
| LDL 3+4 (small dense) | 37 | 26 |
| Remnant lipoprotein (LDL + VLDL3) | 22 | 26 |

## Case Study #2

John was born with an unfortunate genetic trait—a tendency to depression. He became aware of the problem in high school. He felt down for no reason for months at a time. His sadness and anxiety became more pronounced over the years, and in his twenties obsessive-compulsive behaviors emerged.

Depression, anxiety, and obsessive-compulsive behaviors are quite a combination of symptoms. John worked with doctors at Stanford University to come up with a cocktail of medications that would help alleviate the symptoms. The right combination of drugs was hard to find. Although drugs helped, they came with side effects.

With the negative side effects, countless visits to doctors, therapy sessions, and the high daily expense of medications, John got fed up and sought other solutions. While reading the paper one Sunday, he came across an article about the use of ketosis to keep seizures under control. He reasoned that if ketosis helped stabilize the brain against seizures, it might be a tool to help fight depression. Fascinated, he wanted to learn more. He eagerly read research papers and blogs.

While little research had been done on the effects of ketosis to fight depression and anxiety, it was clear that ketosis helps the brain. John shared his findings with his doctor. While public literature only hypothesized about depression and anxiety, he ran his own experiment to see what results he could experience. He tracked his diet and anxiety for two months, moving toward a therapeutic level of ketosis.

For years John had been an on-again, off-again smart-carb eater. He typically had periods of strict compliance followed by sugar binges. He felt that a month of tracking himself at this baseline would be enough time to observe these behaviors and their effects.

One morning, his office had piping-hot bagels. John could not resist the bakery smells wafting through the halls. Two hours after eating those carbs, his anxiety set in. The anxiety was so bad that he contemplated leaving work. This was his first clue. High-starch foods appeared to make his symptoms worse.

Looking at the baseline data from his month of regular eating, it was clear that John felt worst when he was the least compliant with his low-carb diet. In his daily life, cookies had become a type of self-medication. However, through his experimentation, he could see that the momentary improvement in his feelings from eating a bag of cookies was followed by days of negative ripple effects on his mood. As he continued to explore, he began to see a pattern. High-sugar, high-starch foods made him feel worse.

Next, he began to transition to a ketogenic diet, at the same time working with his doctor to reduce medications. What happened? A high-fat diet lowered some of the background anxiety and depression. While his symptoms did not disappear, the big mood swings were eliminated.

John describes himself in his new lifestyle as "much more steady." He hopes that with this change in diet, he can work with his doctor to wean himself off medications entirely. John is both optimistic and realistic about the results. While he is not afraid to use medications "if things get rough," he is pleased to have a lifestyle tool to manage his issues on an ongoing basis. He currently is on less medication with fewer side effects.

Inflammation

# IS YOUR BODY INFLAMED?: C-REACTIVE PROTEIN

Category: **Inflammation, Activity**

Difficulty: **Advanced**

What you need: **Prescription for a blood test**

Cost: **$**

## Why this test

Chronic inflammation is an underlying cause of excess weight. It lays the foundation for heart disease and other chronic illness later in life. The physical effects of acute inflammation can be seen, but detecting chronic inflammation inside the body is more difficult. Data on inflammation levels in the blood can give you this valuable information.

## What you can expect to learn

• Identify levels of inflammation in the body.

## Background

C-reactive protein is found in the blood and rises in response to inflammation in the body. This protein binds to the surface of dead and dying cells. Monitoring this protein is a great way to understand what's happening in your cells. Are they in working order, or are some cells sick and dying? Sick cells cause inflammation that taxes the roadways of your veins and arteries.

Unfortunately, C-reactive protein identifies only the presence of inflammation. It does not tell you the cause. Since high levels of inflammation require more sleuthing to understand, doctors may choose to limit its use for diagnostic purposes. However, a tinkerer can learn a lot from this simple test. Change one variable at a time and see what happens, gathering clues about possible causes. As an added bonus, this test will show you the effects of your healthy-eating efforts. Take the test before and after making changes in your diet to gauge your progress.

## What to do

1. Get a prescription from your doctor.

2. Take the test when healthy to get an accurate baseline reading. Illness or injury throws off the number. Also, hard workouts cause a breakdown of cells, leading to higher levels of inflammation. To avoid skewing your results, get blood drawn before you work out.

## Interpreting the data

The ideal level of C-reactive protein is less than 1 mg/L, but the number will skyrocket when you are sick or hurt. Is your number high even though you are healthy? Eliminate grains, dairy, and legumes from your diet. Incorporate anti-inflammatory foods such as fish. Test again after two weeks. Number still high? Is excess exercise breaking down your body so much that it can no longer repair itself? Adjust the intensity of your physical activity. Take the test again. If your number is still high, seek a health-care professional to work with you to get to the root of the problem.

Inflammation

# IDENTIFYING PROBLEM FOODS: INTOLERANCE/ALLERGY STUDY

Category: **Food, Inflammation**

Difficulty: **Intermediate**

What you need: **Discipline, body awareness, recording method**

Cost: **Free**

## Why this test

Some foods, whether part of a Paleo diet or not, may cause irritation in your system. At the extreme, these foods cause allergies. For most people, though, problem foods cause only low-grade, annoying symptoms, including digestive discomfort, gas, bloating, or pain. Even if your reactions are not severe, consistent low-grade exposure to foods your body doesn't like can cause chronic inflammation.

## What you can expect to learn

- Interpret cues from your body to identify problem-causing foods.
- Determine if foods cause allergies or low-grade stress on your digestive system.
- Identify foods to avoid.

## Background

Grains and legumes that ravage the gut (see page 70) are not the only dietary culprits of inflammation. While some people do fine with dairy, others can't tolerate it. A strict Paleo diet eliminates many of the low-grade food allergens, but as with any diet, you also lose access to foods you enjoy. As you try to find a balance between strict Paleo and a livable middle ground, allergies and discomfort can return with a vengeance.

If you know which foods your body doesn't like, you can avoid them. While doctors offer blood tests to determine allergies, the results are not always reliable. The most effective test is to clean up your diet by omitting all foods that are potential allergens. Once your system has been reset, you can reintroduce foods one at a time. When your body doesn't like something, you will notice. Your body will try to speak to you through symptoms such as gas, bloating, or headaches. Pay attention and adjust your response to your body's needs. While this test does take weeks of discipline, the outcome can give you insight into your ideal diet.

## What to do

1. Commit to an elimination diet for a four- to six-week period.

2. The first seven to twelve days are a detox period of eating only foods that are unlikely to be allergens. Eat only these foods: organic turkey, lamb, squash, sweet potatoes, cauliflower, cabbage, lettuce, cranberries, peaches, pears, olive oil, and filtered water. This means no coffee, tea, alcohol, or other beverages except water.

3. At the end of the detox period, begin to introduce foods back into your diet. Eat the same new food at each meal for one to two days. If you feel a reaction, discontinue it and wait for symptoms to clear before introducing the next food. Common allergens to introduce one at a time include dairy, citrus, shellfish, seafood, beef, refined sugar, peanuts, nuts, eggs, potatoes, corn, rice, tomatoes, soy, bananas, and caffeinated products, including chocolate, tea, coffee, and soda.

As you eat these new foods, record how your body responds. How do you feel? What do you notice? Is your body speaking to you?

## Interpreting the data

Pay attention to all kinds of symptoms during the study. Symptoms may include abdominal pain, cramping, diarrhea, or excess gas. If you experience these symptoms from eating a particular food, you can consider yourself intolerant.

Pain and digestive discomfort are not the only symptoms you may experience. Other symptoms can include:

Skin—itching, burning, hives, red spots, sweating

Ear, nose, and throat—sneezing, runny nose, sore or dry throat, hoarseness, ringing in the ears, dizziness

Respiratory system—wheezing, excess mucous, shortness of breath

Cardiovascular system—increased heart rate or pounding heart, flushing, tingling, faintness

Gastrointestinal system—increased salivation, canker sores, indigestion, bloating, stomachache, heartburn, constipation

Genitourinary system—frequent, urgent, or painful urination; inability to control bladder; itching; discharge; pain; water retention

Musculoskeletal system—fatigue, weakness, pain, swelling, stiffness of joints, backache

Nervous system—headache, migraine, drowsiness, inability to concentrate, depression, irritability, restlessness, hyperactivity, dizziness, numbness, tremors

At the end of the study, you will have a list of safe foods and a list of foods to avoid. Foods you are allergic to cause damage to your body; eliminating foods that your body does not tolerate gives you time to heal. If the food is one you can't live without, try reintroducing it six months later. But be honest with yourself: if your body rejects something, you have to trust it. If you are intolerant of many foods that seem to have little in common, this might be a sign of leaky gut, autoimmune conditions, small intestinal bacterial overgrowth (SIBO), or a gut pathogen. A gut-healing protocol may be in order (see page 216).

Cortisol

# IS YOUR BODY STRESSED?: DAILY CORTISOL PATTERN

Category: **Hormones**

Difficulty: **Intermediate**

What you need: **Prescription for a cortisol test**

Cost: **$$**

## Why this test

Cortisol is the stress hormone that circulates in your body. Acute cortisol elevation is expected from time to time as you encounter challenges in life. Chronically high cortisol, however, can cause stress on your body and make you store fat, especially in your midsection, where abdominal fat cells are particularly sensitive to this hormone.

## What you can expect to learn

* Determine if you are experiencing chronic stress.

## Background

Beyond its function as a fight-or-flight stress hormone, cortisol gets your body moving in the morning. When you're healthy, your cortisol is highest in the morning and then gradually declines throughout the day, reaching its lowest level three or four hours after you fall asleep. If you have a stressful lifestyle, cortisol follows a similar pattern but at much higher levels.

You can test your cortisol level to understand how your body is dealing with the stress of everyday life. You can either have a blood panel done in a lab or collect saliva samples at home throughout the day and mail them to a lab. While a blood test gives you a single snapshot, saliva tests performed over the course of a day will provide a view into your body's trends.

Testing can be done through your doctor or with test kits ordered online. Prices vary widely, so compare before ordering.

## What to do

1. Get a prescription for a cortisol test from your doctor.

2. Take the test over the course of a day.

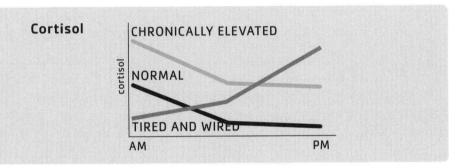

## Interpreting the data

Normal cortisol starts out high in the morning. Levels should taper off by the afternoon and bottom out at bedtime. Chronically high levels of cortisol are often well above normal levels and can indicate problems. Abnormal cortisol patterns start out low and reach a high at the end of the day.

De-stressing is not self-indulgent New Age mumbo jumbo; controlling your base levels of cortisol through stress management is important to your health. Here are some tips to help manage those base levels:

- Say no to drama.

- Minimize exposure to stressful people.

- Eat regularly.

- Limit your consumption of stimulants, like caffeine, to the morning, when cortisol levels are naturally high.

- Practice sitting still.

- Breathe deeply.

- Take a walk.

- Do yoga.

Cortisol, Activity

# OPTIMIZE PERFORMANCE THROUGH SMART RECOVERY: USING RESTWISE TO GET THE MOST OUT OF TRAINING

Category: **Hormones, Activity**

Difficulty: **Intermediate**

What you need: **Restwise software**

Cost: **$$**

## Why this test

Good stressors encourage your body to grow stronger and faster. However, too much of a good thing can be detrimental, causing a lack of performance gains, fatigue, and adrenal failure. The key to continued athletic development is knowing how hard to push yourself without going overboard. Restwise, an online tool, helps you understand the factors of performance and gives you an overall recovery score. You can use this score to inform your training and ensure that you are getting the maximum bang for your training buck.

## What you can expect to learn

* Identify training needs.

* Know when it is time to rest.

* Understand recovery as a score that can be tracked over time.

* See how lifestyle choices can support your performance goals.

* Identify markers that are associated with overtraining.

* Habituate good behaviors that support top performance.

* Gain confidence in training decisions.

## Background

The stress receptors in your body are a blunt tool. They are excellent at sensing stress and sending out hormonal messages to rally your body to action. However, the body does not differentiate well between stressful training and life stress. To your body, stress is stress. If there is not enough of it in training, your body does not get stronger. On the other hand, too much stress impedes your performance. But it can be hard to know when to push, reduce intensity, or rest completely.

Restwise helps you understand recovery. It pulls together several different factors that relate to overtraining, such as hours slept, sleep quality, energy level, mood, training performance, appetite, symptoms of illness, muscle soreness, hydration, and body weight. Restwise algorithms weight the importance of these factors differently and calculate an overall recovery score. This score is a valuable insight into your training and the patterns in your recovery.

While the score is a valuable tool, it offers just a glimpse into what's going on. A low score is an invitation to ask questions about your lifestyle and the factors that stress your body.

The key to using this tool is to use it honestly. It is easy to be aspirational in your answers, knowing what the system needs for a high score. The value, however, is in listening to your body. With a bit of practice, thinking through your score and interpreting what's going on in your body will become second nature. With the score in hand, you'll have data to help you make better training decisions.

## What to do

1. Go to restwise.com and download the software. Commit to the program for at least four weeks.

2. Each day, fill out a 60-second questionnaire about training, rest, soreness, heart rate, weight, and so on.

## Interpreting the data

Use your daily score to inform your training choices. If it's low, dial back the intensity. Identify whether stressors are caused by training or by lifestyle choices. If lifestyle choices are the culprit, make appropriate changes and continue to monitor your score. If training is the problem, rest. Doing so will give your body time to recuperate and come back stronger when it's ready.

Watch your score over time as well. If it worsens, ask yourself what factor resulted in a lower score.

## Case Study

Todd is an athlete and a coach. Over the past two decades, he has trained hard and raced often. He will be participating in his sixth Ironman in Kona, Hawaii, soon. His life is busy and active, and for years he trained religiously six days a week. Each week Todd set a training schedule and stuck to it no matter what. He was disciplined about doing what the schedule told him to do—biking, swimming, running, weight training, intervals.

After battling injuries, surgeries, and recovery from training accidents, Todd sought a new tool to inform his training. He often found himself going through the motions even though he was tired and overworked. He continued to battle injuries. In addition to the fatigue of his training, Todd was diagnosed with multiple sclerosis.

Even with all his health issues, giving up racing was not an option for Todd. He loved it too much. Two years ago, Todd began to incorporate Restwise into his routine. It helped him identify the thin line between stressing his body enough to see gains and improvements and stressing his body too much, thus mitigating gains from his workouts and running down his body.

Each morning Todd takes a minute to fill out the survey that calculates a recovery score. He has found that a score between 60 and 80 works for him. In this range, his workouts are productive—he has consistent energy and sees improvements in his training. When Todd trains hard, his recovery score can dip into the mid-60s. This is a sign that he is pushing his body. But when his score drops into the low 60s or 50s, he knows he is pushing his body too hard. It is time to make changes in his training and lifestyle. For each individual, the ideal recovery score range is different. Some of Todd's athletes who use the tool "fall apart" with recovery scores in the 60s and need to aim for scores in the 80–90 range.

When Todd's numbers are low, he applies common sense by asking a series of questions about his lifestyle and training. What is happening in his life? Is he sleeping enough? Is travel affecting his stress levels? Is he training too hard? On top of his intuitive sense of how he is doing, he applies the objective Restwise number. If his training needs to be dialed back, he varies his workout schedule. Instead of doing a long ride, he might rest, or instead of doing heavy interval training, he will do a light ride.

This upfront data also serves as a helpful tool to set expectations about a training session. Todd knows that if his recovery number is on the low side, he might not perform as well. Conversely, if his recovery score is high, he can push himself hard. With Restwise, his workouts have been more productive. Instead of pushing through periods of fatigue, he takes the time to let his body get stronger.

A sample of the data from Todd's final week of training for the Ironman is on pages 178 and 179.

With difficult training, Todd's score is falling below his benchmark (60) for altering the intensity. Since his workout on the sixteenth was light—just a swim—Todd proceeded with his training as planned. That night he got insomnia, a common sign of overtraining. If not corrected, this can lead to big problems during intense training.

Training on the seventeenth was a four-hour bike ride and a four-mile run at Ironman race pace and effort. This workout was meant to be done in one solid chunk of time, with the run immediately following the bike. However, Todd's Restwise score was low: 48. Instead of pushing through the wall, he opted to skip the workout and start resting a week early.

After two days of rest, Todd attempted a difficult bike ride on the nineteenth. However, his performance was not there. Instead of pushing it, he did an easy ride and took two more days off. His score began to improve on the twenty-third. He did an easy run of 3 miles instead of 5. When the Restwise score goes up again, performance improves. With the body properly rested, a new stage of training can begin with maximum benefits gained.

Beyond the improvements in performance, Todd has noticed other issues while tracking with Restwise. For example, over the past two years, he has experienced some unplanned weight loss. The weight has come off gradually. He postulates that the weight loss is a side effect of one of the medications he takes for multiple sclerosis. Using the long-term data, he has been able to share the information with his doctors to discuss treatment options with less severe side effects.

| Date | Score | Heart Rate | SP02 | Weight | Hours Slept, Including Naps | Sleep Quality | Energy Level |
|------|-------|-----------|------|--------|---------------------------|---------------|--------------|
| 1/10 | 86 | 52 | 96 | 150.4 | 8 | Normal | Normal |
| 1/11 | 87 | 51 | 96 | 149.2 | 8 | Normal | Normal |
| 1/12 | 60 | 48 | 96 | 151.4 | 9.5 | Worse Than Normal | Worse Than Normal |
| 1/13 | 80 | 51 | 96 | 152.8 | 9.5 | Normal | Normal |
| 1/14 | 87 | 47 | 96 | 152 | 7.7 | Better Than Normal | Normal |
| 1/15 | 60 | 49 | 96 | 151.6 | 8.5 | Worse Than Normal | Worse Than Normal |
| 1/16 | 58 | 49 | 96 | 149.8 | 8 | Normal | Worse Than Normal |
| 1/17 | 44 | | | | 4 | Normal | Worse Than Normal |
| 1/18 | 72 | | | | 7 | Worse Than Normal | Normal |
| 1/19 | 46 | | | | 8 | Worse Than Normal | Worse Than Normal |
| 1/20 | 38 | | | | 6 | Worse Than Normal | Worse Than Normal |
| 1/21 | 44 | | | | 8 | Worse Than Normal | Worse Than Normal |
| 1/22 | 57 | 45 | 96 | 153.0 | 8 | Normal | Worse Than Normal |
| 1/23 | 67 | 48 | 96 | 154.4 | 8 | Normal | Worse Than Normal |
| 1/24 | 84 | 55 | 96 | 153.5 | 9 | Better Than Normal | Normal |

| Mood | Yester-day's Training Perfor-mance | Appetite | Illness | Muscle Soreness | Injury | Urine Shade | Comments |
|------|------|------|------|------|------|------|------|
| Normal | Normal | Normal | No | No | No | Yellow | Body Fat% = 4.5 |
| Normal | Normal | Normal | No | No | No | Yellow | BF% = 4.6 |
| Normal | Better Than Normal | Normal | No | Yes | No | Yellow | BF% = 4.2 |
| Normal | Worse Than Normal | Normal | No | No | No | Yellow | BF% = 4.3 |
| Normal | Normal | Normal | No | No | No | Yellow | BF% = 4.4 |
| Normal | Normal | Normal | No | Yes | No | Yellow | BF% = 5 |
| Worse Than Normal | Normal | Normal | No | Yes | No | Pale Yellow | BF% = 4.5 |
| Worse Than Normal | Normal | Less Than Normal | No | No | No | Pale Yellow | away |
| Normal | Rest Day | Normal | No | No | No | Pale Yellow | away |
| Normal | Normal | Normal | No | No | No | Pale Yellow | away |
| Normal | Worse Than Normal | Normal | No | No | No | Pale Yellow | away |
| Normal | Normal | Normal | No | No | No | Pale Yellow | away |
| Worse Than Normal | Rest Day | Normal | No | Yes | No | Pale Yellow | BF %= 4.5 |
| Normal | Rest Day | Normal | No | Yes | No | Pale Yellow | BF %= 5.4 |
| Normal | Normal | Normal | No | No | No | Yellow | BF %= 5.3 |

Cortisol

# CHOOSING THE ACTIVITY THAT IS RIGHT FOR YOUR BODY: CORTISOL RESPONSE TO EXERCISE

Category: **Hormones, Activity**

Difficulty: **Intermediate**

What you need: **Prescription for pre- and post-stressor cortisol tests**

Cost: **$$**

## Why this test

Just as the insulin factories grow weary from overwork, so do the cortisol factories. This effect is called *adrenal fatigue* or *adrenal insufficiency*. When your cortisol factories, the adrenal glands, are not working properly, you are rundown and don't see gains in performance. Understanding how your adrenal glands are functioning can help you choose the activity that will give your body what it needs—whether stimulation to get stronger or rest to recuperate.

## What you can expect to learn

- Identify how your adrenal glands are responding to acute stressors.

- Determine if specific exercises are causing your body more harm than good.

- Identify reasons for feeling rundown and not seeing gains in performance.

- Choose activities that are right for your body now.

## Background

Acute stressors—isolated instances of stress—can be caused by brief confrontations, challenges at the office, blowups at home, or even exercise. You cannot control most of the acute stressors the world throws your way. You can, however, control the stress you give yourself in the form of exercise. The right kind of exercise builds muscle tone, increases insulin sensitivity, lowers blood pressure, strengthens bones, and lowers stress, making you feel good. The wrong kind of exercise adds to already high levels of stress, and the physical benefits come at a cost.

What are the right and wrong types of exercise? Like many issues in health, the answer depends on you and your unique physiology. While lifting hard and heavy is great for some people, yoga is better for others. What is good for you depends on the baseline stress levels in your life, as well as how often and how hard you train, and how long you've been training.

If you have trained hard consistently for years, always pushing for maximum effort or until failure, your cortisol factories might be running on fumes. You have probably seen your performance and fitness levels hit a wall. To see more progress, your adrenal glands have to rest and work within their limits.

Looking at how you feel and perform can be a great starting point for determining if your body is overstressed by the exercise you are inflicting on it. Feeling depressed or lethargic, having no desire to work out, having slow recovery times, finding your performance at a plateau, or, for women, experiencing irregular menstruation are signs that your body is fatigued and your adrenal glands may be overworked.

Testing cortisol before and after a stressor like exercise gives you a view of how your adrenal glands are keeping up. While some doctors charge a hefty $600 to run lab work, online services will do the job for around $200. For instance, BioHealth Laboratory (www.biodia.com) offers an exercise tolerance test with skilled doctors to help you interpret results. If you are an athlete who consistently pushes to the limit, this is a good investment.

## What to do

1. Plan a workout between 4:00 and 8:00 p.m., when your cortisol level should be low.

2. Collect saliva and do one test before your workout.

3. Perform your workout. When finished, do a test one hour after and another one two hours after.

4. Send in your results for processing.

## Interpreting the data

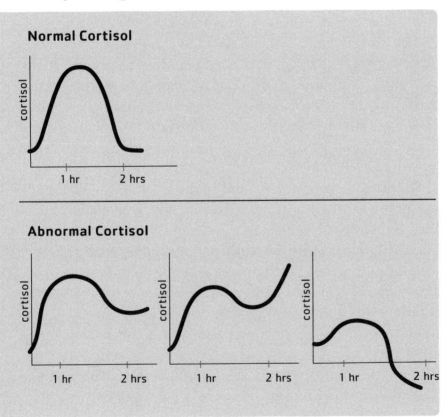

## Normal Cortisol

A normal graph should look like the top one at left. The starting value is your baseline. After exercise, cortisol rises, and then it drops one hour later, returning to baseline two hours after exercise. If your cortisol level drops below your baseline, your exercise decreased stress. Win!

## Abnormal Cortisol

If your graph differs from the normal arc, then your exercise caused more stress or your adrenal glands are fatigued. Your body can react abnormally after a stressor in three different ways:

1. Cortisol can rise without a return to baseline. This response indicates that the type of exercise you are doing is increasing stress instead of decreasing it.

2. Cortisol can rise and then continue to rise. Here the body is responding to the stress as if danger is imminent and it anticipates more stress.

3. Cortisol rises only a little and then dips well below baseline. This response indicates late-stage adrenal fatigue. The body is so tired that it no longer can muster the ability to respond to the stresses demanded of it.

If you respond to an exercise stressor abnormally, take note and consider backing off. Your body is programmed to function in cycles of hard work and rest. Rest gives the body a chance to repair, recover, and grow. You are not designed for constant activity or stress. Exercise is hard work, and you want to make sure that all your effort is doing your body good, not damaging it. Understanding where you are in the work-and-rest cycle is an important part of smart training.

If your adrenal glands are taxed, take a break from intensive exercise for a couple of weeks or months. Instead, choose an activity that doesn't stress your body, such as walking, yoga, or swimming. This lifestyle change does not have to last forever. You can get back to your long bike rides, runs, and heavy lifting soon enough. The rest period will bolster your physiology, giving your body a chance to repair itself and come back even stronger. For those who have made intense exercise a part of daily life, this transition can be hard. Be kind to yourself. Taking a break is not laziness—it's smart training. Ease slowly into your training regimen, and make note of how you feel. If you start to experience adrenal fatigue symptoms again, work with a doctor or other health-care practitioner to explore other possible causes and treatments.

Hormones

# PULL THE PLUG ON STRESS: HEART RATE VARIABILITY AND THE EMWAVE

Category: **Hormones**

Difficulty: **Intermediate**

What you need: **emWave device**

Cost: **$$**

## Why this test

Stress is toxic to the body, the mind, mood, effectiveness, and productivity. When your brain registers stress, it sets off a chain reaction of more than 1,400 biochemical changes, causing, among other things, the stress hormone cortisol to flood the body. While an argument may last only a few minutes, its effect on the body can last six hours. Constant stress hijacks the brain, keeping you in a constant state of fight-or-flight. The results are a domino effect of negative consequences, such as fat storage, increased appetite, high blood pressure, and decreased athletic performance.

Our modern world presents us with constant emotional and physiological stressors. But while the body reads these stressors as death threats, e-mail won't really kill you. Understanding your body's response and knowing how to refocus your emotions can help you pull the plug on stress and make you more effective in everything you do. But counting to ten and meditating are touchy-feely solutions, and while they might slow your heart rate, they do not solve the messaging problem received by your brain.

Learning the language of your body, in this case heart rate variability, enables you to control your reactions to stressors. The emWave can provide concrete, real-time feedback about how you are doing and tools to train your body and mind to keep you calm, productive, and stress-free.

## What you can expect to learn

- Collect real-time data to help you understand your physiological response to stress.

- Learn training methodologies to take charge of your emotional state.

- Find tools to refocus negative emotions and avoid unnecessary stress.

- Embrace a technological anchor for behavior change.

## Background

It's no surprise that the brain tells the body what to do. But the heart also tells the brain what to do. Heart signals sent to the brain have a profound influence on emotional process (feelings) as well as attention, perception, memory, and problem-solving. The brain and body are constantly communicating to keep each other apprised of what is happening in the environment.

When your heart races or gets excited, a message is sent to the emotional center of the brain, the amygdala. Deep in the brain, the amygdala is the body's eavesdropping tool. It looks for incoming sensory information and tries to match those signals (of threats both perceived and actual) with memories of a previous experience. When the amygdala matches incoming information with past experiences of threat, it sets off a series of biochemical changes that prepare the body for fight or flight. In this way, the heart informs the brain's reading of a situation, and the brain mobilizes the body to respond to the stressor. However, if the stressor is not life-threatening, as stressors usually aren't, your body is bombarded with the wrong signals.

The key to breaking the cycle is gaining control of your heart rhythms. This is not to be confused with heart rate. Most people think of heart rate as a metronome, faithfully beating on a steady, regular rhythm. Even under resting conditions, though, the heartbeat is irregular, with varying intervals between beats. This beat-to-beat variation is called *heart rate variability* (HRV). To control the heart's rhythms is to control stress and beat the physiological hijacking caused by your overzealous amygdala.

When your HRV is regularly patterned, your mind is calm. The brain associates this ordered pattern with feelings of security and well-being. This type of rhythm is called *coherence*, and it reinforces positive feelings and emotional stability. If, however, your heartbeat is irregular and incoherent, your amygdala takes over the physiological show and mobilizes the body for a stress response. Learning to generate heart rhythm coherence is the key to unplugging the stress cycle, sustaining positive emotions, and positively affecting the way you perceive, think, feel, and perform.

## What to do

1. Connect the emWave device to your smartphone, tablet, or laptop. Before your first session, watch the online video that explains how to use the product (viewable at www.heartmathstore.com).

2. Attach the sensor to your ear and begin. The sensor will wirelessly transmit real-time data to your device. The goal is to stay in a coherent or green state for as much of your session as possible.

3. Train for 10–15 minutes a day for two weeks. Use the application to see how long you can keep your heart in a coherent state. Learn what it feels like to be in that state.

## Interpreting the data

Learn to change your heart rate variability with real-time feedback using these techniques:

**Focus.** Draw your attention to your heart, pulling awareness into your chest. Breathe. Pay attention to your breath. Observe your breath as it comes in and out. Inhale for five seconds. Exhale for five seconds. Use the tools in the emWave app to time the pacing of your breath.

**Layer positive emotional states.** Appreciation and care are the two emotions that change physiology the most. Think of a calm and peaceful time: playing ball with your kids or spending time on the beach and watching the waves crash on the shore. Reflect on as many details as possible. What does it look like, sound like, feel like? What do you hear? What do you smell? Put yourself in that moment.

**Observe the changes in your body.** What does it feel like to be in a coherent state? How do your heart, body, and mind feel? Practice staying in that state for as long as you can.

Apply what you have learned to everyday situations. Pay attention when you feel a stress response. Disengage at the first onset of stress or elevated heart rate. Focus on your heart and breath, and summon positive emotions. If you use techniques to break the stress cycle and prevent your body from being in a constant state of fighting for survival, you will achieve a productive state for problem-solving and be able to face challenges calmly and with control.

## Case Study

Janet was a good eater most of the time. She focused on whole foods and made conscious efforts to eat healthy. However, when life got stressful, she began to eat processed foods. She couldn't help it. A hard day at work or an emotionally charged encounter with a friend would set off a landslide of bad eating decisions.

Stress drove Janet to polish off a pint of ice cream in one sitting. But that was not enough. She layered on candy, chips, and soda. Normally self-disciplined, Janet felt out of control and unable to stop eating. Her binging was affecting the way she looked and felt. And her binge eating became more frequent, up to three times a week.

Janet's problem wasn't self-discipline; it was stress. High cortisol levels were driving her to eat. To control her eating, Janet had to control the root problem. She ordered an emWave device and started training every morning. After a couple of weeks, she was aware when her heart rate became elevated and a stress reaction was about to begin.

As Janet became more aware of what stress felt like in her body, she could take steps to calm herself before her brain could interpret a little incident as a life threat. Using emWave techniques, she was able to limit stress responses throughout the day. The result was reduced stress baggage when she got home.

On nights when she felt like bellying up to the cupcake bar, she would first take out her emWave device and spend ten minutes training. She reasoned that it was okay to have treats every now and again. However, she needed to be in the right frame of mind before indulging. The emWave tool ensured that she was eating treats for the right reason: as something special and not in response to stress.

Food, Hormones, and Activity

# GET ON TOP OF YOUR HEALTH: THE GRAND-DADDY OF BLOOD WORK, WELLNESSFX

Category: **Food, Hormones, Inflammation, Activity**

Difficulty: **Easy**

What you need: **Access to a lab for a blood draw**

Cost: **$$$**

## Why this test

WellnessFX provides at least fifty diagnostics at a single go. Since it works outside of the health-care system, costs are kept low (less than if you paid cash working with a doctor). You don't have to ask for a prescription, and skilled practitioners are there to help you interpret trends across systems of the body. Doctors coach you in addressing the roots of problems through smart lifestyle recommendations instead of just drugs. WellnessFX offers all this and easy-to-understand, visualized data online.

## What you can expect to learn

* Uncover hidden problems.
* Discover the effects of lifestyle and dietary changes on blood values.
* Get guidance on interpreting results.
* Come away with actionable lifestyle changes.

## Background

The body is a complex system. While most blood tests give a snapshot of a particular marker, getting a holistic sense of what is going on can be difficult. Some doctors may not have the time to sleuth. Patients without an immediate problem can be a lower priority.

Valuable tools are emerging, and the costs are dropping. San Francisco–based WellnessFX runs a comprehensive panel of more than fifty diagnostics ranging from metabolic panels—including thyroid, sex hormones, cardiac, liver, and kidney functions—to vitamins and minerals. Unlike many other testing companies, its goal is not to sell vitamins or drugs. Instead, WellnessFX aims to provide insight and let the data encourage behavior change. Follow-up blood work is done after several months to show the results of your efforts. Panels range in cost from $29 to $599. It is worth making this data a regular part of your health care.

## What to do

1. Sign up online at www.wellnessfx.com. You will be issued a prescription for a blood draw.

2. Have your blood drawn at one of WellnessFX's partner labs.

3. Review your lab results. Easy-to-read and fun-to-engage data is provided online.

4. Schedule a consultation. Make an appointment with a WellnessFX provider to dive into your data and uncover personalized results and recommended lifestyle changes.

5. Retest to see the results of the changes you've made.

## Interpreting the data

When your results are available, you set up phone consultations with knowledgeable doctors who help you sleuth through your personal data and find insights unique to you. Together you map out a plan for lifestyle changes to help address problem areas. When medications or supplements are recommended, physicians work with you so that you can be on the minimum effective dose. These efforts are combined with lifestyle and dietary changes.

## Case Study

James is a CrossFit coach who works out regularly and takes nutrition seriously. He pays careful attention to his diet and eats lots of protein to maintain muscles while limiting carbohydrates.

Even though he is in tip-top shape, James recently took the WellnessFX panel and was surprised by the results. While most athletes would expect high levels of testosterone, his testosterone was low. The levels of testosterone precursor dehydroepiandrosterone (DHEA) mirrored the testosterone results. Low testosterone is a key hormone in muscle growth and repair and fat metabolism. Without enough testosterone, it is impossible to reap the full rewards of a workout. Clearly, even though he was in good health, James had something to improve upon.

Collaborating with WellnessFX doctors, James reviewed his patterns to identify potential causes for this marker. First, they discussed increasing weight lifting to increase testosterone. However, James was already lifting heavy weights three or four times a week. Next, they explored sleep, since poor sleep can decrease testosterone. It was clear that James takes his sleep seriously and makes sure to get more than adequate rest. Finally, they discussed diet. James shared his diligence in eating protein and limiting carbs. Problem solved. Limited fat intake was constraining the formation of testosterone. James upped his consumption of healthy dietary fats, saw changes in his testosterone level, and broke through a performance plateau.

# QUICK REFERENCE GUIDE

You may be just now getting your carbs and diet under control. Or you may be further along on the journey—tweaking glucose, testing cortisol, and cycling in and out of intense exercise. Where you are on the path doesn't matter as long as you are moving toward health. Once you start testing and see what's going on in your body firsthand, you gain motivation from feeling healthier while simultaneously seeing your results improve.

The chart on the following page is organized by the pillars for optimal health. It can help you understand how each component can be tested, monitored, and changed. The rows are organized from easiest lifestyle changes to those that require a doctor's order.

| Food | Hormones INSULIN | Hormones CORTISOL | Inflammation | Activity |
|---|---|---|---|---|
| Eat nature's foods to increase nutrition and fill the body up with good carbohydrates | Eat nature's foods to help cells become more sensitive to insulin | Eat nature's foods to limit excess stress response from food | Replace egregious carbs with nature's foods to limit and fight inflammation | |
| Limit fruit and fructose | Sleep more to increase insulin sensitivity | Limit stress | | Incorporate activity into daily life |
| Limit carbs | Eat low-carb foods that do not spike glucose and insulin, avoiding a cortisol kick | | | Fuel activity with nutrient-dense carbs for energy |
| Count carbs (see page 105) | | Sleep in a blacked-out room to reduce stress | | |
| Eat Paleo: meats, vegetables, nuts, seeds, little starch, little fruit, no sugar | Eat fat and protein to limit food's effects on blood sugar | | Eat Paleo to avoid grains that cause inflammation | Eat Paleo to maximize performance and recovery |
| Determine optimal level of carbohydrates (see page 108) | Test HbA1c (see page 130) | Take a daily cortisol level test (see page 171) | Test C-reactive protein to measure inflammation markers in the body (see page 166) | Fuel smartly during your post-workout fueling window (see page 89) |
| | Test bedtime glucose (see page 119) | | Perform elimination test to identify food allergens (see page 168) | Take pre- and post-stressor tests to determine effect on cortisol levels (see page 180) |
| | Test glucose after meals (see page 124) | | | Test adrenal function (see page 171) |
| | Perform a glucose tolerance test (see page 126) | | | |

easy ↑

difficult ↓

# PART IV

## A PRACTICAL GUIDE FOR YOUR PERSONALIZED DIET

Putting it all together

## Chapter 7

# PRIMAL MEAL PLANS FOR A MODERN WORLD

## A day-by-day guide to what to eat

You thrive when you eat quality foods designed by nature. But many variations of a "good" diet exist based on your goals and the foods your body can tolerate. For some, losing weight might be a priority; for others, it may be performance or managing an autoimmune disease or allergies. The key to success is to take general diet principles and then personalize them based on your body, needs, and lifestyle.

These sample menus and accompanying recommended self-tests show you how to tweak the basic plan based on your goals and what you track. Start with Squeaky Clean Paleo. If that goes well, consider adding dairy. If you are experiencing digestive problems, however, consider starting with a restorative diet like GAPS (see page 216) to set you up for success with a whole-foods diet.

If you add dairy to your Paleo diet, listen to your body. Give it what it needs, not what it craves. Responding to your body smartly will set up good habits.

## TIPS FOR SUCCESSFUL PALEO EATERS

**Don't be afraid to eat the same meals.** Having a set breakfast makes morning decision-making easy. Have a quick meal that you eat Monday through Friday. You will know how long it takes to prepare, and starting your day right will become routine.

**Prepare meals in batches.** Gaining momentum to cook can be the hardest part of meal prep. Dedicate a couple nights a week to preparing meals for later. Pack your lunches for several days. Making several meals at once also saves on clean-up time.

**Make extra for leftovers.** When preparing meals, make extra portions to save or freeze. Having standbys in the fridge is a great way to avoid diet derailments when you are ravenous or your schedule gets hectic. Eat leftovers for a quick breakfast, or pack them for lunch.

## WHERE TO GO ON THE WEB FOR GREAT PALEO RECIPES

Against All Grain (againstallgrain.com)

Balanced Bites (balancedbites.com)

Civilized Caveman Cooking Creations (civilizedcavemancooking.com)

The Clothes Make the Girl (theclothesmakethegirl.com)

Everyday Paleo (everydaypaleo.com)

The Food Lovers Kitchen (primalpalate.com)

Nom Nom Paleo (nomnompaleo.com)

Paleo Comfort Foods (paleocomfortfoods.com)

PaleOMG (paleomg.com)

Paleo Parents (paleoparents.com)

Paleo Spirit (paleospirit.com)

The Whole Kitchen (thewholekitchen.com)

# SQUEAKY CLEAN PALEO 12-DAY MEAL PLAN

When you eat the natural foods your body is designed to eat, you have consistent energy throughout the day. You look and feel great. It's not a sacrifice. Here's how.

**What to eat:** Meats, vegetables, nuts, seeds, some starch, some fruit

**What to avoid:** Sugar, artificial sweeteners, grains, dairy

**Self-tests you might consider (see Part III):**

- Your Body's Response to Diet: End-of-Day Glucose Testing
- The Body's Glucose Tracker: HbA1c
- How to Improve Your Cholesterol in Two Weeks Without Drugs
- Is Your Body Inflamed?: C-Reactive Protein
- Gaining Control of Your Appetite: Tracking the Important Hormonal Messenger Leptin

## Day 1

**Breakfast:** Scrambled eggs cooked in 1 tablespoon ghee and steamed spinach

**Lunch:** Salad of mixed greens with wild-caught canned salmon

**Dinner:** Hamburger wrap (hamburger, tomato, onion, and avocado, wrapped in romaine lettuce), cabbage slaw, and homemade oven-roasted sweet potato fries

## Day 2

**Breakfast:** Frittata with mixed vegetables

**Lunch:** Bacon-wrapped chicken thighs and chopped salad of cucumbers, tomatoes, red onions, and avocado with balsamic vinaigrette

**Dinner:** Herbed chicken, green beans, and side salad with balsamic vinaigrette

## Day 3

**Breakfast:** Steamed asparagus topped with poached eggs

**Lunch:** Chopped chicken salad (chicken, celery, grapes, green onions, walnuts, and homemade mayonnaise)

**Dinner:** Beef and vegetable stir-fry served over cauliflower "rice"

## Day 4

**Breakfast:** Egg "muffins" (eggs cooked in muffin pan with bacon and onions)

**Lunch:** Chicken breast, grilled peach wrapped in prosciutto, and salad of mixed greens with balsamic vinaigrette

**Dinner:** Grilled scallops, grilled asparagus, and heirloom tomato salad with basil

## Day 5

**Breakfast:** Scrambled eggs cooked in 1 tablespoon ghee and steamed kale

**Lunch:** Lamb or beef stew

**Dinner:** Lemon rosemary chicken with roasted zucchini, carrots, and red bell peppers, and blueberry crumble made with almond flour and honey

## Day 6

**Breakfast:** Grain-free granola

**Lunch:** Chicken soup with zucchini, carrots, and onions

**Dinner:** Spaghetti squash with meatballs and tomato sauce

## Day 7

**Breakfast:** Omelet with mixed vegetables

**Lunch:** Flank steak salad with balsamic vinaigrette

**Dinner:** Taco salad (hamburger, guacamole, salsa, chopped lettuce, and red and orange bell peppers)

## Day 8

**Breakfast:** Soft-boiled eggs, steamed vegetables, and slice of ham

**Lunch:** Cobb salad of grilled chicken breast, avocado, hard-boiled eggs, chopped tomatoes, olives, and bacon with balsamic vinaigrette

**Dinner:** Cabbage cooked in chicken broth with dill, sausage, side salad with balsamic vinaigrette, and fruit

## Day 9

**Breakfast:** Eggs scrambled with bacon, onions, bell peppers, and zucchini

**Lunch:** Wild-caught canned salmon with lemon juice, served on cucumber slices

**Dinner:** Stuffed bell peppers with meat and herbs, and salad of mixed greens with balsamic vinaigrette

## Day 10

**Breakfast:** Sausage, eggs fried in ghee, and roasted tomato

**Lunch:** Ham, crudités with eggplant dip, and salad of mixed greens with balsamic vinaigrette

**Dinner:** T-bone steak topped with whipped herb butter, broccoli, and salad of mixed greens with balsamic vinaigrette

## Day 11

**Breakfast:** Sweet potato hash with baked egg on top

**Lunch:** Egg salad wrapped in romaine lettuce and salad of mixed greens with balsamic dressing

**Dinner:** Pork tenderloin, mashed cauliflower, and green beans sautéed in ghee

## Day 12

**Breakfast:** Breakfast casserole with spicy sausage

**Lunch:** Taco salad (chicken breast, guacamole, onions, salsa, and chopped cilantro)

**Dinner:** Turkey burgers and cabbage slaw

# WEIGHT LOSS 12-DAY MEAL PLAN

When your body is functioning properly and your hormonal messengers (leptin and insulin) are working the way they should, you are satisfied. You do not crave foods that are bad for you, and you have steady energy throughout the day. This plan limits carbohydrates and focuses on tasty meals made from real foods—no more starving yourself skinny.

**What to eat:** Proteins, non-starchy vegetables (such as kale, broccoli, cauliflower, and spinach), healthy fats (ghee, olive oil, coconut oil, lard)

**What to avoid:** Starchy vegetables (roots), fruit, dairy, alcohol, desserts (even if Paleo-friendly)

**Self-tests you might consider (see Part III):**

- Recalibrating Your Carb-O-Meter: Counting Carbs to Reset Normal

- Your Body's Response to Diet: End-of-Day Glucose Testing

- The Body's Glucose Tracker: HbA1c

- Gaining Control of Your Appetite: Tracking the Important Hormonal Messenger Leptin

## Day 1

**Breakfast:** Scrambled eggs cooked in 1 tablespoon butter and sautéed spinach

**Lunch:** Salad of mixed greens and wild-caught canned salmon

**Dinner:** Hamburger wrap (hamburger, tomato, onion, avocado, and homemade mayonnaise wrapped in lettuce), cabbage slaw, and sautéed kale

## Day 2

**Breakfast:** Breakfast frittata with mixed vegetables

**Lunch:** Bacon-wrapped chicken thighs and chopped salad of cucumbers, tomatoes, red onions, and avocado with balsamic vinaigrette

**Dinner:** Herbed chicken and green beans sautéed in lard, garnished with shallots fried in lard

## Day 3

**Breakfast:** Steamed asparagus topped with poached eggs

**Lunch:** Chopped chicken salad (chicken, celery, grapes, walnuts, and homemade mayonnaise)

**Dinner:** Beef and vegetable stir-fry served over cauliflower "rice"

## Day 4

**Breakfast:** Egg "muffins" (eggs cooked in muffin pan with bacon and onions)

**Lunch:** Club wrap (chicken breast with bacon, tomatoes, avocado, homemade mayonnaise, and mustard, wrapped in romaine lettuce)

**Dinner:** Grilled scallops, grilled asparagus, and heirloom tomato salad with basil and balsamic vinaigrette

## Day 5

**Breakfast:** Scrambled eggs cooked in 1 tablespoon ghee, bacon, and kale sautéed in chicken broth

**Lunch:** Grilled halibut fillet, olive tapenade, and salad of mixed greens with balsamic vinaigrette

**Dinner:** Pork tenderloin, Brussels sprouts, and side salad

## Day 6

**Breakfast:** Grain-free granola

**Lunch:** Egg salad wrapped in romaine lettuce and salad of mixed greens with balsamic vinaigrette

**Dinner:** Spaghetti squash with tomato sauce and meatballs

## Day 7

**Breakfast:** Omelet with mixed vegetables

**Lunch:** Flank steak salad with balsamic vinaigrette

**Dinner:** Taco salad (hamburger, tomatoes, guacamole, salsa, chopped lettuce, and red and orange bell peppers)

## Day 8

**Breakfast:** Soft-boiled eggs and leftover vegetables

**Lunch:** Cobb salad (grilled chicken breast, avocado, hard-boiled eggs, chopped tomatoes, olives, and bacon with balsamic vinaigrette)

**Dinner:** Lamb or beef stew

## Day 9

**Breakfast:** Scrambled eggs cooked in 1 tablespoon ghee and steamed spinach

**Lunch:** Leftover stew

**Dinner:** Lemon rosemary chicken and roasted zucchini, carrots, and red bell peppers

## Day 10

**Breakfast:** Eggs Benedict–style poached egg and sliced country ham served on a bed of steamed spinach with hollandaise sauce

**Lunch:** Thanksgiving wrap (turkey, cranberry sauce, lettuce, tomatoes, onions, and homemade mayonnaise, wrapped in romaine lettuce)

**Dinner:** Sausage, steamed cauliflower, and Brussels sprouts sautéed in ghee

## Day 11

**Breakfast:** Sausage with eggs fried in ghee

**Lunch:** Nitrate-free deli meat, pâté, and crudités

**Dinner:** T-bone steak topped with whipped herb butter, broccoli, and salad of mixed greens with balsamic vinaigrette

## Day 12

**Breakfast:** Eggs scrambled with bacon, onions, bell peppers, and zucchini

**Lunch:** Wild-caught canned salmon with lemon juice, served on cucumber slices

**Dinner:** Red bell peppers stuffed with meat and herbs, and salad of mixed greens with balsamic vinaigrette

# ATHLETIC PERFORMANCE 12-DAY MEAL PLAN

Fueling for athletes varies depending on individual goals and training. Endurance athletes have different carbohydrate needs than Olympic weight lifters. This meal plan focuses on increased carbohydrates and energy-dense foods. Use self-testing to help determine optimal levels for your body and level of activity.

**What to eat:** Protein, nutrient-dense foods (sweet potatoes and other root vegetables), animal fats, dairy, probiotics to help with digestion (sauerkraut, kimchi, kombucha)

**What to avoid:** Alcohol, low-quality protein powders

**Post-workout:** Eat cooked sweet potatoes or other nutrient-dense carbohydrates within 20 minutes of a tough workout

**Self-tests you might consider (see Part III):**

- Optimizing Carbs: Assessing How You Look, Feel, and Perform to Refine Carb Intake

- Choosing the Activity That Is Right for Your Body: Cortisol Response to Exercise

- Get on Top of Your Health: The Granddaddy of Blood Work, WellnessFX

## Day 1

**Breakfast:** Scrambled eggs cooked in butter, bacon, and spinach sautéed in butter

**Lunch:** Mixed greens salad with wild-caught canned salmon

**Snack:** Homemade trail mix

**Dinner:** Hamburger wrap (hamburger, tomatoes, avocado, and onions, wrapped in lettuce), cabbage slaw, and sweet potato fries

## Day 2

**Breakfast:** Breakfast frittata with mixed vegetables

**Lunch:** Bacon-wrapped chicken thighs and chopped salad of cucumbers, tomatoes, red onions, avocado, and balsamic vinaigrette

**Snack:** Hard-boiled eggs

**Dinner:** Herbed chicken, green beans, and roasted broccoli and root vegetables (sweet potatoes, carrots, turnips, parsnips, rutabagas)

## Day 3

**Breakfast:** Steamed asparagus topped with poached eggs

**Lunch:** Chopped chicken salad (chicken, celery, grapes, green onions, walnuts, and homemade mayonnaise)

**Post-workout:** Sweet potato recovery shake (½ cup sweet potato mash, 1 cup whole milk, 2 egg whites, ⅛ teaspoon cinnamon, 1 pinch nutmeg, 1 pinch ground ginger, 1 pinch allspice, branched-chain amino acids, L-glutamine, R-lipoic acid)

**Dinner:** Beef and vegetable stir-fry served over cauliflower "rice"

## Day 4

**Breakfast:** Egg "muffins" (eggs cooked in muffin pan with bacon and onions)

**Lunch:** Salad of roasted chicken, sweet potatoes, shallots, and mixed greens

**Snack:** Salami and cheese

**Dinner:** Grilled scallops, heirloom tomato salad with basil and balsamic vinaigrette, and grilled sweet potatoes with lime and cilantro dressing

## Day 5

**Breakfast:** Sweet potato hash with baked egg on top

**Lunch:** Egg salad wrapped in romaine lettuce and salad of mixed greens with balsamic vinaigrette

**Snack:** Trail mix granola bar

**Dinner:** Pork tenderloin, sweet potato "linguine" with sage and butter sauce, and salad of mixed greens with balsamic vinaigrette

## Day 6

**Breakfast:** Grain-free granola, bacon, and full-fat yogurt

**Lunch:** Grilled salmon or halibut fillet, olive tapenade, and salad of mixed greens with balsamic vinaigrette

**Endurance workout:** Sweet potato energy gel during endurance training (1 cup mashed sweet potato, ½ cup coconut milk, 1 cup orange juice, juice of one lime, juice of one lemon, and salt)

**Dinner:** Spaghetti squash with tomato sauce, meatballs, and Parmesan cheese

## Day 7

**Breakfast:** Omelet with mixed vegetables

**Lunch:** Taco salad (hamburger, guacamole, sour cream, salsa, chopped lettuce, and red and orange bell peppers)

**Snack:** Beef jerky

**Dinner:** Halibut with sweet potato salsa and steamed broccoli with ghee

## Day 8

**Breakfast:** Poached eggs over asparagus sautéed in ghee and topped with hollandaise sauce

**Lunch:** Cobb salad (grilled chicken breast, tomatoes, olives, avocado, hard-boiled eggs, boiled fingerling or Yukon potatoes, blue cheese, and balsamic vinaigrette)

**Snack:** Hard-boiled eggs

**Dinner:** Lamb or beef stew, squash, and salad of mixed greens with balsamic vinaigrette

## Day 9

**Breakfast:** Sweet potato pancakes topped with fruit preserves and coconut milk whipped cream

**Lunch:** Leftover stew, side salad with herbed buttermilk dressing, and almond crackers

**Snack:** Roasted sweet potato cubes

**Dinner:** Lemon rosemary chicken and roasted zucchini, carrots, and red bell peppers

## Day 10

**Breakfast:** Eggs Benedict–style poached egg with sliced ham served on a bed of steamed spinach and topped with homemade hollandaise sauce

**Lunch:** Thanksgiving wrap (turkey, cranberry sauce, tomatoes, onions, and homemade mayonnaise, wrapped in romaine lettuce)

**Snack:** Butternut squash soup topped with sour cream or crème fraîche

**Dinner:** One-pan scramble of sliced sausage, kale, sliced sweet potatoes, onions, and zucchini

## Day 11

**Breakfast:** Leftover sausage, fried eggs, and cauliflower "latkes"

**Lunch:** Turkey chili with sweet potatoes substituted for beans

**Snack:** Canned lemon-pepper tuna

**Dinner:** T-bone steak topped with whipped herb butter, steamed broccoli with butter topped with shallots fried in butter or lard, and beet salad with feta cheese and walnuts on a bed of greens

## Day 12

**Breakfast:** Eggs scrambled with bacon, onions, bell peppers, and zucchini

**Lunch:** Wild-caught canned salmon with lemon juice, served on cucumber slices

**Snack:** Crudités with hummus, eggplant, or roasted red pepper dip

**Dinner:** Sweet potatoes stuffed with meat and herbs, side salad with balsamic vinaigrette, and grain-free zucchini nut bread

# KETOGENIC 12-DAY MEAL PLAN

The goal with this meal plan is a ratio of 1 carbs to 2 protein to 8 fat. The number of grams of each micronutrient is calculated based on the protein requirements for your lean body mass. This sample menu is meant to expose you to general meal ideas. Calculate your own nutritional needs and personalize proportions for your body type and weight.

You can start by calculating your daily protein requirement. The amount of daily protein you need is based on your body weight. To maintain muscle mass, you need 0.36 grams of protein per pound of body weight. The basic formula is:

**Your weight x 0.36 = grams of protein you should aim to eat each day**

For example, if you weigh 150 pounds, your protein intake should be 150 x 0.36 = 54 grams a day. If you weigh 200 pounds, aim for 72 grams of protein a day.

**What to eat:** Protein, healthy fats (ghee, animal fats, cold-pressed olive oil, coconut oil), medium-chain triglyceride (MCT) oil

**What to avoid:** Overconsumption of protein, energy-dense carbs (root vegetables, fruit, alcohol)

**Self-tests you might consider (see Part III):**

* Learning from a Fat-Filled Diet: Experiments in Ketosis

* How to Improve Your Cholesterol in Two Weeks Without Drugs

* Gaining Control of Your Appetite: Tracking the Important Hormonal Messenger Leptin

* Get on Top of Your Health: The Granddaddy of Blood Work, WellnessFX

## Day 1

**Breakfast:** Eggs fried in ghee, chopped onions, bacon, dollop of crème fraîche, coffee with heavy cream, MCT oil dressing (2 tablespoons MCT oil, 1 tablespoon cold-pressed olive oil, dash of balsamic vinegar; take it plain or serve on top of salad)

**Lunch:** Halibut with dill butter, cauliflower sautéed in ghee, and salad with blue cheese and full-fat dressing

**Snack:** Celery sticks with cream cheese

**Dinner:** Steak pan-fried in ghee with a dollop of butter, and mushrooms and broccoli sautéed in butter

## Day 2

**Breakfast:** Two whole eggs plus one egg yolk fried in ghee, butter lettuce salad with MCT oil dressing, and coffee with heavy cream

**Lunch:** Cobb salad (chicken, bacon, avocado, and hard-boiled eggs with full-fat blue cheese dressing)

**Snack:** Full-fat Greek yogurt topped with olive oil and dash of balsamic vinegar

**Dinner:** Pork chop baked in garlic cream and shredded cabbage with dill sautéed in ghee

## Day 3

**Breakfast:** Protein shake (cream, almond milk, pure protein powder, frozen berries) and butter lettuce salad with MCT oil dressing

**Lunch:** Keto tacos (ground meat, shredded cheddar cheese, sour cream, salsa, and taco spices served on romaine lettuce)

**Snack:** Cream cheese with almond flour crackers

**Dinner:** Chicken with Parmesan cheese, spinach with onions and garlic sautéed in butter, and herbed salad with full-fat dressing

## Day 4

**Breakfast:** Chorizo breakfast casserole (baked eggs, chorizo, onion, heavy cream, spinach, and cheddar cheese) and salad with MCT oil dressing

**Lunch:** Salad of flank steak, guacamole, sour cream, shredded cheese, cilantro, mixed greens, and full-fat dressing

**Snack:** Bone broth (cooked with meat only, no vegetables)

**Dinner:** Keto chili (ground turkey, bacon, onions, celery, green bell peppers, and tomatoes, topped with sour cream, shredded cheese, and hot sauce)

## Day 5

**Breakfast:** Sausage, eggs fried in ghee with crème fraîche, salad with MCT oil dressing, and coffee with heavy cream

**Lunch:** Tuna (canned in oil) with diced hard-boiled egg, celery, and homemade mayonnaise, wrapped in romaine lettuce

**Snack:** Hard cheese

**Dinner:** Pork tenderloin, Brussels sprouts sautéed in butter or lard, and salad of mixed greens with full-fat dressing

---

## Day 6

**Breakfast:** Two whole eggs plus one egg yolk fried in ghee, butter lettuce salad with MCT oil dressing, and coffee with heavy cream

**Lunch:** Duck confit salad with vinaigrette dressing

**Snack:** Can of herring or mackerel in oil

**Dinner:** Grilled steak with bone marrow, creamed spinach, and salad of mixed greens with full-fat dressing

---

## Day 7

**Breakfast:** Protein shake (cream, almond milk, pure protein powder, frozen berries) and butter lettuce salad with MCT oil dressing

**Lunch:** Taco salad (hamburger, guacamole, salsa, chopped lettuce, and red and orange bell peppers)

**Snack:** Cream cheese wrapped in sliced roast beef

**Dinner:** Prosciutto-wrapped halibut with sage butter, chard sautéed in lard with bacon, and salad of mixed greens with full-fat dressing

---

## Day 8

**Breakfast:** Poached egg over steamed asparagus with homemade hollandaise sauce

**Lunch:** Cobb salad (strips of chicken breast sautéed in butter, tomatoes, olives, bacon, hard-boiled eggs, and red bell peppers with full-fat blue cheese dressing)

**Snack:** Herbed cream cheese on almond crackers

**Dinner:** Chicken breast stuffed with cheddar cheese, fried jalapeños stuffed with cream cheese and wrapped in bacon, and salad of mixed greens with herbs and balsamic vinaigrette

## Day 9

**Breakfast:** Cheese omelet and mixed greens salad with MCT oil dressing

**Lunch:** Leftover stuffed chicken breast

**Snack:** Cream cheese and celery

**Dinner:** Grilled sausage, cabbage sautéed in butter or lard, and herbed salad with vinaigrette

## Day 10

**Breakfast:** Poached egg with sliced country-style ham on a bed of steamed spinach with hollandaise sauce

**Lunch:** Chicken salad (chicken, homemade mayonnaise, celery) served in romaine lettuce leaves and cheddar cheese

**Snack:** Pâté on cucumber slices

**Dinner:** Slow-roasted pork belly with fennel and rosemary, salad of mixed greens with full-fat yogurt dressing

## Day 11

**Breakfast:** Sausage, eggs fried in butter, steamed broccoli, and salad of mixed greens with MCT oil dressing

**Lunch:** Chicken salad with chopped tomatoes, cucumbers, feta, and olives

**Snack:** Almond crackers with herbed cream cheese dip

**Dinner:** T-bone steak topped with whipped herb butter, asparagus with hollandaise sauce, and salad of mixed greens with herb dressing

## Day 12

**Breakfast:** Keto pancakes (made from nut flour) with butter, scrambled eggs, and greens with MCT oil

**Lunch:** Salad Niçoise (grilled ahi tuna, olives, greens, and balsamic vinaigrette)

**Snack:** Cream cheese and celery

**Dinner:** Baked chicken legs with herbed yogurt sauce, kimchi, and salad of mixed greens

# TROUBLESHOOTING YOUR GUT: WHAT TO DO ABOUT DIGESTIVE DIFFICULTIES WHEN SWITCHING TO PALEO

Common problems and how to prepare your system for a whole-foods diet

## WHAT DO I DO IF I FEEL CRAPPY EVEN WHEN I EAT RIGHT?

For some people, transitioning to a Paleo diet is painful. Large amounts of fiber from vegetables can act like sandpaper on a wounded gut, causing digestive discomfort, pain, and bloating. Even after making the switch, many people continue to experience uncomfortable gastrointestinal symptoms such as diarrhea, bloating, constipation, abdominal pain, and heartburn. The diet isn't bad; your gut is injured. Your gut needs time to heal before it can do the hard work of processing nature's foods in their basic forms.

Problems with the gut can be the result of several issues—imbalances in gut flora, severe gut wall inflammation, or leaky gut. Before your body is able to receive whole foods, you may need to follow a healing diet aimed at rebuilding the gut walls and repopulating healthy microbes.

# COMMON PROBLEMS WHEN SWITCHING TO A PALEO DIET

If the transition to Paleo is difficult and painful, chances are that problems exist that need to be addressed. Seek the help of a knowledgeable practitioner to walk you through the healing process. In some cases, diet alone can't help. In others, a more gentle diet aimed at tightening the junctions between cells in the gut and repairing breaches, all while rebalancing the microbial flora, might do the trick. A gut-healing diet may be in order for a month. See the day-by-day guide in the menu section. Here are a few common problems with the gut.

**Fungus overgrowth** *Candida albicans*, a type of fungus, is part of a healthy functioning gut. However, when populations get out of control or migrate to places *Candida* shouldn't be, problems arise. Overgrowth of this fungus can be caused by antibiotic use, diets high in carbohydrates, and high stress. Symptoms include skin and fungal issues, autoimmune issues, diarrhea, bloating, constipation, craving large amounts of sugar, mental fog, and difficulty focusing. A shift to a low-carb diet is the key to eliminating this fungus and starving the yeast from what feeds it—sugar. If problems persist, seek a prescription for Diflucan or Nystatin. If you are self-treating, you can take a supplement of caprylic acid, which comes from coconut oil and weakens the wall of yeast cells, causing them to die. Probiotics also work to restore a healthy balance of gut flora.

**Small intestinal bacterial overgrowth (SIBO)** Bacteria live mostly in the large intestine. However, at times they can migrate to the small intestine and proliferate there, causing a range of uncomfortable symptoms. Many practitioners see an overlap between SIBO and irritable bowel syndrome. Controlling these good bacteria gone rogue can be difficult. If you suspect that you have SIBO, seek a diagnosis. Testing is done through a hydrogen breath test. Doing the right thing isn't obvious. Eating a Paleo diet, with all of its fiber, or taking probiotics that are helpful at other times, could feed the rogue bacteria and worsen symptoms. Some practitioners suggest switching to a restorative diet, such as the Gut and Psychology Syndrome (GAPS) diet, before going full Paleo.

**Fructose malabsorption (FM)** FM is a digestive disorder in which fructose is not properly absorbed in the small intestine. The result is excess fructose in the gut. When it's not absorbed properly, fructose makes its way to the large intestine, where it is fermented by bacteria. This can lead to bacteria overgrowth in the small intestine (see "SIBO," above), bloating, excess gas, and motility issues of the bowels. FM is tested for with a hydrogen breath test. It's recommended that those with FM follow a FODMAP (fermentable oligo-, di-, and monosaccharides and polyols) diet, which avoids:

- fructose (fruits, honey, high-fructose corn syrup)

- fructans (wheat, onions)

- lactose (milk, sugar)

- polyols (sugar alcohols like sorbitol, xylitol, and mannitol, along with fruits such as apples, pears, and plums)

- galactooligosaccharides (legumes, beans, Brussels sprouts, onions)

If you suspect you have FM, try eliminating FODMAP foods from your diet, or undergo the elimination diet outlined in Part III in Identifying Problem Foods.

**Low acid production** The stomach is the digestive system's first stop. When you eat, your stomach is stimulated to produce digestive enzymes, including hydrochloric acid and pepsin. These enzymes help break down food so that the body can easily absorb nutrients. If you suffer from impaired acid production, your food is not fully broken down. Large undigested particles make it into the gut, where they putrefy, causing heartburn, bloating, and other digestive issues. Large protein molecules also enter the bloodstream, causing inflammation.

The causes of low acid production include overpopulation of *H. pylori,* a bacteria that suppresses stomach acid; antacid drugs, which reduce the secretion of hydrochloric acid; and stress. To restore acid production, you have to fix the root of the problem. Get tested for *H. pylori.* Avoid antacids. Manage chronic stress. And help your body ramp up hydrochloric acid production by taking supplements—including hydrochloric acid and pepsin—for three to six months, until you can gradually work your way off of them.

# HOW TO HEAL AND SEAL YOUR GUT

For many of these conditions, a restorative diet helps repair and rebalance the gut. Following a diet full of amino acids, gelatin, glucosamines, fats, vitamins, and minerals heals the gut lining and reintroduces beneficial bacteria. This protocol is based on the GAPS diet.

For complete information on the GAPS diet, refer to:

*GAPS Guide: Simple Steps to Heal Bowels, Body and Brain, Second Edition*, by Baden Lashkov (available at www.badenlashkov.com)

*Gut and Psychology Syndrome: Natural Treatment for Autism, Dyspraxia, A.D.D., Dyslexia, A.D.H.D., Depression, Schizophrenia* by Natasha Campbell-McBride

*Internal Bliss: GAPS Cookbook* (available at GAPSdiet.com)

How fast you move through the stages of this restorative diet depends on you and your body. People with severely compromised guts will spend weeks or months in a single stage, while those who have minor issues can move through the stages quickly. As you introduce new foods, watch for changes in your body. If negative side effects such as cramping, diarrhea, or constipation occur, eliminate the problem food. Continue with the diet for three or four more days and then try introducing the problem food again. In this way, you can move through the stages of the diet at your body's speed.

## GAPS RECOMMENDED FOODS

(ADAPTED FROM *GAPS GUIDE*)

Almonds, including almond butter and oil

Apples

Apricots, fresh or dried

Artichokes

Asiago cheese

Asparagus

Avocados, including avocado oil

Bananas (ripe only, with brown spots on the skin)

Beef, fresh or frozen

Beets

Berries, all kinds

Black, white, and red pepper (ground peppercorns)

Blue cheese

Bok choy

Brazil nuts

Brie cheese

Broccoli

Brussels sprouts

Butter

Cabbage

Camembert cheese

Canned fish, in oil or water only

Capers

Carrots

Cashews, fresh only

Cauliflower

Cayenne pepper

Celeriac

Celery

Cellulose, in supplements

Cheddar cheese

Cherries

Chicken, fresh or frozen

Cinnamon

Coconut, fresh or dried (shredded), without additives

Coconut milk

Coconut oil

Coffee, weak and freshly made, not instant

Collard greens

Colby cheese

Coriander, fresh or dried

Cottage cheese, uncreamed (dry curd)

Cucumber

Dates, fresh or dried, without additives (not soaked in syrup)

Dill, fresh or dried

Duck, fresh or frozen

Eggplant

Eggs, fresh

Fish, fresh or frozen

Garlic

Ghee, homemade (many store varieties contain forbidden ingredients)

Ginger root, fresh

Goose, fresh or frozen

Gorgonzola cheese

Gouda cheese

Grapefruit

Grapes

Hazelnuts

Herbal teas

Herbs, fresh or dried, without additives

Honey, natural

Juices, freshly pressed from permitted fruits and vegetables

Kale

Kiwis

Lemons

Lettuce

Limes

Mangoes

Meats, fresh or frozen

Melons

Monterey Jack cheese

Muenster cheese

Mushrooms

Mustard seeds, pure powder, without any forbidden ingredients

Nectarines

Nut flour or ground nuts (usually ground blanched almonds)

Nutmeg

Nuts, all kinds, freshly shelled; not roasted, salted, or coated (any roasting must be done at home)

Olive oil, virgin, cold-pressed

Olives preserved without sugar or other forbidden ingredients

Onions

Oranges

Papayas

Parmesan cheese

Parsley

Pears

Peas, dried split and fresh green

Pecans

Peppers (bell; green, yellow, red, and orange)

Pheasant, fresh or frozen

Pickles, without sugar or other forbidden ingredients

Pineapple, fresh

Pork, fresh or frozen

Poultry, fresh or frozen

Prunes, dried without additives or in their own juice

Pumpkin

Quail, fresh or frozen

Raisins

Rhubarb

Roquefort cheese

Romano cheese

Shellfish, fresh or frozen

Spices, single and pure, without additives

Spinach

Squash (summer and winter)

Stilton cheese

String beans

Swiss cheese

Tangerines

Tea, weak, freshly made, not instant

Tomato purée, pure, without additives apart from salt

Tomato juice, without additives apart from salt

Tomatoes

Turkey, fresh and frozen

Turnips

Ugli fruit

Vinegar

Walnuts

Watercress

Wine, dry red or white

Yogurt, homemade, fermented for 24 hours at correct temperature

Zucchini

# GETTING READY

This gut-healing diet contains large amounts of soothing and healing bone broths, homemade fermented vegetables, and kefir. Before you begin, make several batches of broth and freeze the extras. Purchase a thermos to take broth with you on-the-go. Gather recipes, jars, and starters for fermented vegetables. Learn how to make kefir.

## HOW TO MAKE BONE BROTH

Bone broth, which is different from meat broth or stock, is simple to make, nourishing, and healing, especially for an inflamed gut. In addition to its soothing qualities, bone broth is great as an electrolyte drink and helps eliminate cravings. Make big batches. Do not use store-bought stocks, granules, or bouillon cubes; they are highly processed and full of detrimental ingredients, and they do not heal the gut. Instead, find a local butcher who has bones and joints from pastured animals.

You can use bones from any animal. Put raw or precooked bones in a pot and fill the pot with water, covering the bones. To help leach minerals from the bones, add a splash of vinegar, apple cider, or lemon juice. Bring to a boil. If you're using whole bones, simmer for 30 hours. If you're using bones that are smashed or cut in half by the butcher, simmer for 12 hours. Bone broth can also be made in a slow cooker. You can have a batch cooking on the counter at all times.

Add Celtic sea salt, which is unprocessed whole salt that contains a higher percentage of mineral-dense natural brine (seawater). Drink bone broth hot or cold. Freeze in individual portions for convenience.

## HOW TO MAKE SAUERKRAUT

Fermented vegetables are an ancient digestive and detoxifying remedy. They are full of beneficial enzymes and bacteria that assist with digestion. While you can buy sauerkraut and other fermented vegetables at the store, they are easy to make at home.

1. Wash one medium-sized head of cabbage and remove the outer leaves.

2. Slice the cabbage thinly and place in a bowl.

3. Wash, peel, and shred 2 carrots and add to the cabbage (optional).

4. Sprinkle with Celtic sea salt to taste.

5. If you like, add dill seeds, seaweed, juniper berries, caraway seeds, black peppercorns, or other spicy seeds.

6. With your hands, knead the mixture well to extract the juices.

7. Pack the mixture, including the juice, into a 1- to 2-quart glass jar, leaving at least 2 inches of space at the top (the cabbage will expand with fermentation).

8. Press firmly to eliminate trapped air.

9. If the juice does not fully cover the cabbage, add salt water until the cabbage is covered.

10. Seal the jar with a tight-fitting lid.

11. Leave the jar in a cool, dark place for 5–7 days while fermentation takes place. Remove any cabbage that makes its way above the brine line and any mold that may appear.

12. Taste-test after a week. The texture and flavor will change as fermentation occurs. It can take several weeks to reach its full flavor. When the sauerkraut is to your taste, place it in the fridge.

## HOW TO MAKE KEFIR AND YOGURT

The right balance of beneficial bacteria in your gut helps keep bad yeasts and bacteria under control. Kefir, a fermented dairy, contains these beneficial yeasts and bacteria. When introducing dairy, try goat milk first, as it is gentlest on the system. If it's tolerated, add cow and sheep milk. Kefir can be made in a warm thermos, oven, or yogurt maker.

1. In a saucepan, bring 4 cups milk close to a boil, stirring occasionally. This step helps destroy any bacteria lingering in the milk. Do not boil the milk, which would affect its structure and taste.

2. Remove the saucepan from the heat. Allow the milk to cool to 105°F–113°F.

3. Add kefir starter. Kefir starter is made in a couple of ways. Dissolve packaged kefir or yogurt starter (available at health food stores) in a couple of tablespoons of milk and then add it to the warmed milk, or add 1/3 cup starter from a previous kefir batch. Pour into a clean, dry thermos, yogurt maker, or jar.

4. Set the kefir aside in a warm place such as a oven or yogurt maker (105–113°F) and let it ferment for at least 24 hours.

5. Place a cheesecloth-lined colander over a bowl. Pour the kefir into the colander and let the excess liquid drip through the cheesecloth. This liquid can be used as a starter for other fermented foods or added to broths, soups, or freshly pressed juices. For a softer yogurt, let the kefir drip for less time. For a thicker consistency, let it drip longer.

# GAPS 30-DAY DIET PLAN

This is a suggested day-by-day plan. How fast you move through the stages will depend on your body, how much healing you need, and which foods you can tolerate. If this diet seems repetitive, it is. It is designed to gradually expose your body to new foods over several days. There is a lot of initial food prep. However, meals are repeated and used in clusters to reduce time spent in the kitchen.

What to make ahead of time: Homemade broths (chicken and beef) and fermented vegetables (see page 221)

---

## Day 1

**Breakfast:** Chicken soup (broth with small chunks of chicken boiled in broth)

**Lunch:** Chicken soup

**Snack:** Cup of broth

**Dinner:** Chicken soup

---

## Day 2

Add carrots cooked in broth to the soup.

**Breakfast:** Chicken soup (broth with chicken and carrots)

**Lunch:** Chicken soup

**Snack:** Cup of broth

**Dinner:** Chicken soup

---

## Day 3

Add zucchini cooked in broth to the soup.

**Breakfast:** Chicken soup (broth with chicken, carrots, and zucchini)

**Lunch:** Chicken soup

**Snack:** Cup of broth

**Dinner:** Chicken soup

---

## Day 4

Add cauliflower cooked in broth to the soup.

**Breakfast:** Chicken soup (broth with chicken, carrots, zucchini, and cauliflower)

**Lunch:** Chicken soup

**Snack:** Cup of broth

**Dinner:** Chicken soup

---

## Day 5

Add to the soup pumpkin cooked in broth and 1 teaspoon juice from homemade fermented vegetables.

**Breakfast:** Chicken soup (broth with chicken, carrots, zucchini, cauliflower, pumpkin, and 1 teaspoon juice from homemade fermented vegetables)

**Lunch:** Chicken soup

**Snack:** Cup of broth

**Dinner:** Chicken soup

---

## Day 6

Add onions cooked in broth to the soup. Introduce beef broth for variety. Increase the amount of fermented vegetable juice in every cup of soup and broth to 2 teaspoons.

**Breakfast:** Chicken soup (broth with chicken, carrots, zucchini, cauliflower, pumpkin, onions, and 2 teaspoons juice from fermented vegetables)

**Lunch:** Chicken soup

**Snack:** Cup of broth with 2 teaspoons juice from fermented vegetables

**Dinner:** Beef soup (broth with beef, carrots, zucchini, cauliflower, pumpkin, onions, and 2 teaspoons juice from fermented vegetables)

## Day 7

Add broccoli cooked in broth to the soup.

**Breakfast:** Chicken soup (broth with chicken, carrots, zucchini, cauliflower, pumpkin, onions, broccoli, and 2 teaspoons juice from fermented vegetables)

**Lunch:** Beef soup (broth with beef, carrots, zucchini, cauliflower, pumpkin, onions, broccoli, and 2 teaspoons juice from fermented vegetables)

**Snack:** Cup of broth with 2 teaspoons juice from fermented vegetables

**Dinner:** Chicken soup

## Day 8

Add cabbage cooked in broth to the soup.

**Breakfast:** Chicken soup (broth with chicken, carrots, zucchini, cauliflower, pumpkin, onions, broccoli, cabbage, and 2 teaspoons juice from fermented vegetables)

**Lunch:** Chicken soup

**Snack:** Cup of broth with 2 teaspoons juice from fermented vegetables

**Dinner:** Beef soup (broth with beef, carrots, zucchini, cauliflower, pumpkin, onions, broccoli, cabbage, and 2 teaspoons juice from fermented vegetables)

## Day 9

Add leeks cooked in broth to the soup.

**Breakfast:** Chicken soup (broth with chicken, carrots, zucchini, cauliflower, pumpkin, onions, broccoli, cabbage, leeks, and 2 teaspoons juice from fermented vegetables)

**Lunch:** Beef soup (broth with beef, carrots, zucchini, cauliflower, pumpkin, onions, broccoli, cabbage, leeks, and 2 teaspoons juice from fermented vegetables)

**Snack:** Cup of broth with 2 teaspoons juice from fermented vegetables

**Dinner:** Chicken soup

## Day 10

Increase probiotics to 3–5 teaspoons per cup of soup and broth. Add a raw egg yolk to the soup at dinner.

**Breakfast:** Chicken soup (broth with chicken, vegetables, and 3–5 teaspoons juice from fermented vegetables)

**Lunch:** Beef soup (broth with beef, vegetables, and 3–5 teaspoons juice from fermented vegetables)

**Snack:** Cup of broth with 3–5 teaspoons juice from fermented vegetables

**Dinner:** Chicken soup (broth with chicken, vegetables, 3–5 teaspoons juice from fermented vegetables, and egg yolk)

## Day 11

If you can tolerate eggs, add a raw egg yolk to every cup of soup and broth. For lunch and dinner, you can eat meat and vegetables cooked in broth on the side. When not having soup, drink a cup of broth fortified with 3–5 teaspoons juice from fermented vegetables at every meal.

**Breakfast:** Chicken soup (broth with chicken, vegetables, 3–5 teaspoons juice from fermented vegetables, and egg yolk)

**Lunch:** Beef soup (broth with beef, vegetables, 3–5 teaspoons juice from fermented vegetables, and egg yolk)

**Snack:** Cup of broth with 3–5 teaspoons juice from fermented vegetables and egg yolk

**Dinner:** Beef with boiled vegetables, cup of broth with 3–5 teaspoons juice from fermented vegetables and egg yolk

## Day 12

Continue to add new broths, such as fish, and more boiled and varied vegetables.

**Breakfast:** Chicken with boiled vegetables, cup of broth with 3–5 teaspoons juice from fermented vegetables and egg yolk

**Lunch:** Beef chunks and vegetables, cup of broth with 3–5 teaspoons juice from fermented vegetables and egg yolk

**Snack:** Cup of broth with 3–5 teaspoons juice from fermented vegetables and egg yolk

**Dinner:** Fish soup (broth with fish, vegetables, 3–5 teaspoons juice from fermented vegetables, and egg yolk)

## Day 13

If you can tolerate eggs, add a soft-boiled egg to the soup and broth. Whites should be cooked, and yolks should remain runny. Add roasted vegetables topped with ghee (clarified butter) and other meats high in animal fat (beef, chicken, lamb).

**Breakfast:** Chicken soup (broth with chicken, vegetables, 3–5 teaspoons juice from fermented vegetables, and soft-boiled egg)

**Lunch:** Beef soup (broth with beef, vegetables, 3–5 teaspoons juice from fermented vegetables, and soft-boiled egg)

**Snack:** Cup of broth with 3–5 teaspoons juice from fermented vegetables and soft-boiled egg

**Dinner:** Beef topped with dollop of ghee and served with a side of roasted vegetables, cup of broth with 3–5 teaspoons juice from fermented vegetables and soft-boiled egg

## Day 14

Add fresh herbs and a small amount of homemade sour cream to the soup, choosing a sample diet from Days 1–13.

## Day 15

Introduce homemade kefir to one meal daily.

**Breakfast:** Chicken soup (broth with chicken, vegetables, 3–5 teaspoons juice from fermented vegetables, soft-boiled egg, herbs, sour cream, and homemade kefir)

**Lunch:** Beef soup (broth with beef, vegetables, 3–5 teaspoons juice from fermented vegetables, soft-boiled egg, sour cream, and herbs)

**Snack:** Cup of broth with 3–5 teaspoons juice from fermented vegetables and soft-boiled egg

**Dinner:** Beef topped with a dollop of ghee and served with a side of roasted vegetables, cup of broth with 3–5 teaspoons juice from fermented vegetables and soft-boiled egg

## Day 16

Add mashed avocado to every bowl of soup, choosing a sample diet from Days 1–13.

## Day 17

Introduce sauerkraut and other fermented vegetables (homemade kimchi; fermented carrots, radish slices, or red cabbage; apple kraut) on the side, starting with 1 teaspoon per meal, choosing a sample diet from Days 1–13.

## Days 18–19

Increase fermented vegetables to 2 teaspoons per meal, choosing a sample diet from Days 1–13.

## Day 20

Add roasted and grilled meats (avoid charred or darkened bits), and increase the amount of fermented vegetables at every meal.

**Breakfast:** Chicken soup (broth with chicken, vegetables, 3–5 teaspoons juice from fermented vegetables, soft-boiled egg, herbs, sour cream, and homemade kefir)

**Lunch:** Grilled steak, cauliflower "rice," fermented vegetables, cup of plain broth

**Snack:** Cup of broth with 3–5 teaspoons juice from fermented vegetables and soft-boiled egg

**Dinner:** Roasted chicken and bell peppers, fermented vegetables, cup of broth with 3–5 teaspoons juice from fermented vegetables and soft-boiled egg

## Day 21

Add 1–2 teaspoons cold-pressed olive oil to dinner, along with lettuce and other raw vegetables.

**Breakfast:** Chicken soup (broth with vegetables, 3–5 teaspoons juice from fermented vegetables, soft-boiled egg, herbs, sour cream, and homemade kefir)

**Lunch:** Grilled chicken breast and vegetables, cup of broth with 3–5 teaspoons juice from fermented vegetables and soft-boiled egg

**Snack:** Cup of broth with 3–5 teaspoons juice from fermented vegetables and soft-boiled egg

**Dinner:** Roasted chicken and bell peppers; butter lettuce salad with cold-pressed olive oil, olives, parsley, and tomatoes; cup of broth with 3–5 teaspoons juice from fermented vegetables and soft-boiled egg

## Day 22

Add 1–2 teaspoons cold-pressed olive oil to every meal.

**Breakfast:** Soft-boiled eggs, 1–2 teaspoons cold-pressed olive oil, fermented vegetables, cup of plain broth

**Lunch:** Cobb salad (boiled chicken breast, avocado, tomatoes, olives, 1–2 teaspoons cold-pressed olive oil), cup of broth with 3–5 teaspoons juice from fermented vegetables and soft-boiled egg

**Snack:** Plain broth with fermented vegetables on the side

**Dinner:** Roasted lamb shank with broccoli sautéed in garlic ghee; fermented vegetables; butter lettuce salad with 1–2 teaspoons cold-pressed olive oil, olives, dill, and parsley; cup of broth with 3–5 teaspoons juice from fermented vegetables and soft-boiled egg

## Day 23

**Breakfast:** Eggs scrambled with onions and peppers, fermented vegetables, 1–2 teaspoons cold-pressed olive oil, cup of plain broth

**Lunch:** Grilled flank steak over salad with 1–2 teaspoons cold-pressed olive oil, fermented vegetables, cup of plain broth

**Snack:** Cup of broth with 3–5 teaspoons juice from fermented vegetables and soft-boiled egg

**Dinner:** Roasted lamb shank with broccoli sautéed in garlic ghee, fermented vegetables, butter lettuce salad with 1–2 teaspoons cold-pressed olive oil and herbs, cup of plain broth

## Day 24

Add homemade nut bread (grain-free bread made with nut flour).

**Breakfast:** Nut bread, scrambled eggs, homemade kefir, cup of broth, fermented vegetables

**Lunch:** Chicken salad (diced chicken, avocado, cucumbers, red bell peppers, cilantro, and squeeze of lime) with a dollop of homemade sour cream, fermented vegetables, cup of broth with 3–5 teaspoons juice from fermented vegetables and soft-boiled egg

**Snack:** Cup of broth with 3–5 teaspoons juice from fermented vegetables and soft-boiled egg

**Dinner:** Bell peppers stuffed with ground beef and herbs, sauerkraut, cup of broth with 3–5 teaspoons juice from fermented vegetables and soft-boiled egg

## Day 25

**Breakfast:** GAPS granola (pumpkin seeds, sunflower seeds, coconut flakes, honey, cinnamon, vanilla extract) with homemade kefir, scrambled eggs cooked in plenty of ghee, cup of broth with 3–5 teaspoons juice from fermented vegetables and soft-boiled egg, 2 teaspoons cold-pressed olive oil

**Lunch:** Leftover stuffed bell peppers, sauerkraut, cup of broth, salad of mixed greens with cold-pressed olive oil

**Snack:** Cup of broth with 3–5 teaspoons juice from fermented vegetables and soft-boiled egg

**Dinner:** Lamb in coconut curry served over cauliflower "rice," fermented vegetables, butter lettuce salad with herbs and balsamic vinaigrette, cup of broth

## Day 26

**Breakfast:** Nut bread; egg casserole with shredded cheddar cheese, cooked sausage, chopped onions, bell peppers, cauliflower, and dollop of homemade crème fraîche; cup of broth with 3–5 teaspoons juice from fermented vegetables

**Lunch:** Waldorf salad (romaine lettuce, chopped turkey, celery, apples, pecans, red grapes, and homemade mayonnaise)

**Snack:** Cup of broth with 3–5 teaspoons juice from fermented vegetables and soft-boiled egg

**Dinner:** Grilled steak with a dollop of ghee, salad of tomatoes and avocado splashed with olive oil and salt, cup of broth with 3–5 teaspoons juice from fermented vegetables and soft-boiled egg

## Day 27

**Breakfast:** Nut bread, scrambled eggs cooked in lots of ghee, cup of broth with 3–5 teaspoons juice from fermented vegetables and soft-boiled egg

**Lunch:** Salad of romaine lettuce, tomatoes, bacon (farm-fresh, home-cured), and avocado with cold-pressed virgin olive oil and balsamic vinaigrette; cup of broth with 3–5 teaspoons juice from fermented vegetables and soft-boiled egg

**Snack:** Cup of broth with 3–5 teaspoons juice from fermented vegetables and soft-boiled egg

**Dinner:** Beef topped with a dollop of ghee and served with roasted and fermented vegetables, cup of broth with 3–5 teaspoons juice from fermented vegetables and soft-boiled egg

## Day 29

**Breakfast:** GAPS granola, cup of broth with 3–5 teaspoons juice from fermented vegetables and soft-boiled egg

**Lunch:** Butternut squash soup, cup of broth with 3–5 teaspoons juice from fermented vegetables and soft-boiled egg

**Snack:** Cup of broth with 3–5 teaspoons juice from fermented vegetables and soft-boiled egg; deviled eggs

**Dinner:** Turkey chili (no beans), salad with homemade dressing, fermented vegetables, cup of broth

## Day 30

**Breakfast:** Scrambled eggs cooked in lots of ghee, sausage, fermented vegetables, berries with a dollop of crème fraîche, cup of broth

**Lunch:** Butternut soup with a dollop of crème fraîche, roasted chicken breast, cup of broth, salad of mixed greens with cold-pressed olive oil

**Snack:** Cup of broth with 3–5 teaspoons juice from fermented vegetables and soft-boiled egg

**Dinner:** Flank steak salad, fermented veggies, cup of broth

## Day 31 and Beyond

Continue to drink broths and eat fermented vegetables and homemade fermented dairy, including kefir, crème fraîche, and sour cream, as well as other healthy fats—oils and avocados. As your gut symptoms improve, gradually add other foods and transition into a full Paleo diet.

## QUICK TIPS FOR KEEPING A HEALTHY GUT

**Eat gut-healing bone broths.** Homemade broths are full of nutrition that supports healthy gut walls and tight cell junctions and provides the raw materials needed to keep the body strong. Make bone broth a part of your regular diet and cooking routine. It is a comforting food that is great on its own or as a base for soups. If making soups on a regular basis is too difficult, consider supplementing with gelatin.

**Don't get hooked on antacids.** It is easy to pop pills, but they often resolve symptoms without addressing underlying problems. An overreliance on antacids can impair the body's natural process of acid production. Seek to eat right. If you need digestive aids to help reboot stomach acid, use them as a temporary solution, not a long-term fix.

**Be mindful of yeast overgrowth when you take antibiotics.** Take care that opportunistic yeasts and microbes don't overpopulate your system when you take antibiotics. Avoid eating sugar, which can lead to the growth of bad yeasts, and take probiotics that help repopulate the good guys.

# BIBLIOGRAPHY

## PART I: SMART FOODS

### CHAPTER 1: Designed for a Different World

Bellman, E. "Indonesia is all over this problem like white on rice." *Wall Street Journal,* Apr 12, 2011.

Boyd-Orr, J. B., and J. L. Gilks. Studies of *Nutrition: The Physique and Health of Two African Tribes.* London: His Majesty Stationery Office, Medical Research Council No 155, 1931.

Carrera-Bastos, P., M. Fontes-Villalba, J. O'Keefe, S. Lindeberg, and L. Cordain. "The Western diet and lifestyle and diseases of civilization." *Research Reports in Clinical Cardiology 2* (Mar 2011): 15–35.

Catlin, George. (1844). *Letters and Notes on Manners, Customs, and Conditions of North American Indians,* Vol. 1–2. New York: Reprinted Dover Publications, 1971.

Cordain, Loren. *The Paleo Diet.* New York: John Wiley & Sons, Inc., 2002.

Diamond, Jared. "The worst mistake in the history of the human race." *Discover Magazine,* May 1987.

Hrdlicka, Ales. *Physiological and Medical Observations among the Indians of Southwestern United States and New Mexico.* Washington, DC: Washington Printing Office, 1908.

Huang, J., J. Song, F. Qiao, and K. Fuglie. "Sweetpotato in China: Economic aspects and utilization in pig production." CIRAD Agriculture Research for Development (2007).

Lindeberg, Staffan. *Food and Western Disease.* West Sussex, UK: John Wiley & Sons, Ltd., 2010.

Meikle, James, and Luke Harding. "Denmark bans Kellogg's vitamins." *The Guardian*, Aug 12, 2004.

Price, Weston A. *Nutrition and Physical Degradation*. Lemon Grove, CA: Price-Pottenger Nutrition Foundation, Inc., 1939.

Rabagliati, Andrea. *Air, Food and Exercises: An Essay on the Predisposing Causes of Disease*. London: Baillière, Tindall & Cox, 1897.

Rae, John. *John Rae's Correspondence with the Hudson's Bay Company on Arctic Exploration*, 1844–1855. Hudson Bay Record Society, 1953.

Sisson, Mark. *The Primal Blueprint*. Malibu, CA: Primal Nutrition, Inc., 2011.

Stackpole, E. A., cur. The Long Arctic Search: The Narrative of Lieutenant Frederick Schwatka, U.S.A. 1878–1880. Mystic, CT: The Marine Historical Society, 1965.

Stefánsson, Vilhjalmur. *The Friendly Arctic*. New York: Macmillan, 1921.

Taubes, Gary. *Good Calories, Bad Calories*. New York: Anchor Books, 2007.

Volek, Jeff S., and Stephen D. Phinney. *The Art and Science of Low Carbohydrate Living*. Miami, Florida: Beyond Obesity, 2011.

Wolf, Robb. *The Paleo Solution: The Original Human Diet*. Las Vegas, NV: Victory Belt Publishing, 2010.

# PART II:
# STOP SURVIVING, START THRIVING

## CHAPTER 2:
### Food: Not All Calories Are Created Equal

Atwater, W. O. "The potential energy of food. The chemistry and economy of food." *Century Magazine* 34 (1887): 397–405.

Avena, N. M., P. Rada, and B. G. Hoebel. "Evidence for sugar addiction: behavioral and neurochemical effects of intermittent, excessive sugar intake." *Neuroscience Behavioral Review 32*, no. 1 (2008): 20–39.

Boden, G., S. Sargrad, C. Homko, M. Mozzoli, and P. Stein. "Effect of a low-carbohydrate diet on appetite, blood glucose levels, and insulin resistance in obese patients with type 2 diabetes." *Annals of Internal Medicine* 142, no. 6 (2005): 403–11.

Dekker, M., Q. Su, C. Baker, A. Rutledge, and K. Adeli. "Fructose: A highly lipogenic nutrient implicated in insulin resistance, hepatic steatosis, and the metabolic syndrome." *American Journal of Physiology–Endocrinology and Metabolism* 299, no. 5 (Nov 2010): E685–E694.

Gerstein, H., K. Swedberg, J. Carlsson, J. McMurray, et al. "The hemoglobin A1c level as a progressive risk factor for cardiovascular death, hospitalization for heart failure, or death in patients with chronic heart failure." *Archives of International Medicine* 168, no. 15 (Aug 11, 2008): 1699–1704.

Hudgins, L. C. "Effect of high-carbohydrate feeding on triglyceride and saturated fatty acid synthesis." *Society for Experimental Biology and Medicine* 225, no. 3 (Dec 2000): 178–83.

Katz, J. D., S. Agrawal, and M. Velasquez. "Getting to the heart of the matter: Osteoarthritis takes its place as part of the metabolic syndrome." *Current Opinion in Rheumatology* 22, no. 5 (Sep 2010): 512–19.

Kemp, Robert. "Carbohydrate addiction." *Practitioner* 190 (Mar 1963): 358–64.

Macaulay, David. *The Way We Work*. New York: Houghton Mifflin, 2008.

Mayes, P. A. "Intermediary metabolism of fructose." *American Journal of Clinical Nutrition* 58, no. 5 (Nov 1993): 754S–765S.

Nicolls, M. R. "The clinical and biological relationship between Type II diabetes mellitus and Alzheimer's disease." *Current Alzheimer Research* 1, no. 1 (Feb 2004): 47–54.

Parks, E., and M. Hellerstein. "Carbohydrate-induced hypertriacylglycerolemia: Historical perspective and review of biological mechanisms." *American Journal of Clinical Nutrition* 71, no. 2 (Feb 2000): 412–33.

Phinney, Stephen D. "Ketogenic diets and physical performance." *Nutrition & Metabolism* 1, no. 1 (Aug 17, 2004): 2.

Pollan, Michael. *The Botany of Desire*. New York: Random House, 2001.

Sakai, M., M. Oimomi, and M. Kasuga. "Experimental studies on the role of fructose in the development of diabetic complications." *Kobe Journal of Medical Science* 48, no. 5 (Dec 2002): 125–36.

Savage, D., and R. Semple. "Recent insights into fatty liver, metabolic dyslipidaemia and their links to insulin resistance." *Current Opinion in Lipidology* 21, no. 4 (Aug 2010): 329–36.

Stanhope, K. L., and P. J. Havel. "Endocrine and metabolic effects of consuming beverages sweetened with fructose, glucose, sucrose or high-fructose corn syrup." *American Journal of Clinical Nutrition* 88, no. 6 (Dec 2008): 1733S–37S.

Stanhope, K. L., J. M. Schwarz, N. L. Keim, S. C. Griffen, et al. "Consuming fructose-sweetened, not glucose-sweetened, beverages increases visceral adiposity and lipids and decreases insulin sensitivity in overweight/obese humans." *Journal of Clinical Investigation* 119, no. 5 (May 2009): 1322–34.

Taubes, Gary. *Why We Get Fat and What to Do About It*. New York: Alfred A. Knopf, 2011.

Vogelstein, Fred. "Epilepsy's big fat miracle." *New York Times Magazine* (Nov 17, 2010).

Volek, J., S. Phinney, C. Forsythe, E. Quann, et al. "Carbohydrate restriction has a more favorable impact on the metabolic syndrome than a low-fat diet." *Lipids* 44, no. 4 (Apr 2009): 297–309.

Westman, E. C., W. S. Yancy, J. C. Mavropoulos, M. Marquart, and J. R. McDuffie. "The effects of low-carbohydrate, ketogenic diet versus a low-glycemic index diet on glycemic control in type 2 diabetes mellitus." *Nutrition and Metabolism* 19, no. 5 (Dec 2008): 36.

Wikipedia. (n.d.). "Relative sweetness of sugars and sweeteners." Data from Image:Relativesweetness.jpg, en.wikipedia.org/wiki/Fructose.

# CHAPTER 3:
## Hormones: Managing the Body's Traffic Signals

Bado, A., S. Levasseur, S. Attoub, S. Kermorgant, J. P. Laigneau, et al. "The stomach is a source of leptin." *Nature* 394 (Aug 20, 1998): 790–93.

Collins, M. and G. Gibson. "Probiotics, prebiotics, and synbiotics: Approaches for modulating the microbial ecology of the gut." *American Journal of Clinical Nutrition* 69, no. 5 (May 1999): 1052s–1057s.

Druce, M. R., C. J. Small, and S. R. Bloom. "Minireview: Gut peptides regulating satiety." *Endocrinology* 145, no. 6 (June 2004): 2660–65.

Gautron, L., and J. Elmquist. "Sixteen years and counting: An update on leptin in energy balance." *Journal of Clinical Investigation* 121, no. 6 (June 2011): 2087–93.

Jönsson, T., S. Olsson, B. Ahrén, T. Bøg-Hansen, A. Dole, and S. Lindeberg. "Agrarian diet and diseases of affluence—do evolutionary novel dietary lectins cause leptin resistance?" *BMC Endocrine Disorders* 5 (Dec 10, 2005): 10.

Knight, Z. A., K. S. Hannan, M. L. Greenberg, and J. M. Friedman. "Hyperleptinemia is required for the development of leptin resistance." *PLOS ONE* 5, no. 6 (Jun 2010): e11376.

Knutson, K. L. "Impact of sleep and sleep loss on glucose homeostasis and appetite regulation." *Sleep Medicine Clinics* 2, no. 2 (Jun 2007): 187–97.

Kohara, K., M. Ochi, Y. Tabara, T. Nagai, et al. "Leptin in sarcopenic visceral obesity: Possible link between adipocytes and myocytes." *PLOS ONE* 6, no. 9 (2011): e24633.

Li, Min-Dian. "Leptin and beyond: An odyssey to the central control of body weight." *Yale Journal of Biology and Medicine* 84, no. 1 (Mar 2011): 1–7.

Mix, H., A. Widjaja, O. Jandl, M. Cornberg, et al. "Expression of leptin and leptin receptor isoforms in the human stomach." *Gut* 47, no. 4 (Oct 2000): 481–86.

Murphy, K., and S. Bloom. "Gut hormones and the regulation of energy homeostasis." *Nature* 444 (Dec 2006): 854–59.

Patel, S. R., A. Malhotra, D. P. White, D. Gottlieb, and F. Hu. "Association between reduced sleep and weight gain in women." *American Journal of Epidemiology* 164, no. 10 (Nov 2006): 947–54.

Rastall, R., G. Gibson, H. Gill, F. Guarner, et al. "Modulation of the microbial ecology of the human colon by probiotics, prebiotics and synbiotics to enhance human health: An overview of enabling science and potential applications." *FEMS Microbiology Ecology* 52 (Apr 2005): 145–152.

Rosedale, Ron. "Insulin, leptin, and the control of aging." Slides from author website. 2006. www.drrosedale.com/resources/pdf/Ron-Rosedale-Talk-on-Insulin-Leptin-and-the-Control-of-Aging.pdf

---. "Leptin—its essential role in health, disease, and aging." www.drrosedale.com/resources/pdf/Leptin and its essential role in health disease and aging.pdf.

---. "Insulin and its metabolic effects." 1988. www.drrosedale.com/resources/pdf/Insulin and Its Metabolic Effects.pdf.

Ropelle, D., M. Flores, D. Cintra, G. Rocha, et al. "IL-6 and IL-10 anti-inflammatory activity links exercise to hypothalamic insulin and leptin sensitivity through IKKbeta and ER stress inhibition." *PLOS Biology* 8, no. 8 (Aug 2010): e1000465.

Sanders, M. E. "Probiotics: Considerations for human health." *Nutrition Reviews* 61, no. 3 (Mar 2003): 91–99.

Saxena, P., A. Prakash, and A. Nigam. "Efficacy of 2-hour post glucose insulin levels in predicting insulin resistance in polycystic ovarian syndrome with infertility." *Journal of Reproductive Technology* 4, no. 1 (Jan–Apr 2011): 20–22.

Spiegel, K., E. Tasali, P. Penev, and E. Van Cauter. "Sleep curtailment in healthy young men is associated with decreased leptin levels, elevated ghrelin levels, and increased hunger and appetite." *Annals of Internal Medicine* 141, no. 11 (Dec 7, 2004): 846–50.

Wiley, T. S., with Bent Fomby. *Lights Out: Sleep, Sugar, and Survival.* New York: Pocket Books, 2000.

World Health Organization. "Health and nutritional properties of probiotics in food including powder milk with live lactic acid bacteria. Report of a joint FAO/WHO expert consultation on evaluation of health and nutritional properties of probiotics in food including powder milk with live lactic acid bacteria." Oct 2001.

## CHAPTER 4:
## Inflammation: When Food Becomes Foe

Bell, S. and D. Clark. "Saccharomyces boulardii: Time for change in the age of cost-effective medicine." *Journal of Nutrition & Food Sciences* 2 (2012): 10. www.omicsonline.org/2155-9600/2155-9600-2-e117.pdf.

Bengmark, S. "Advanced glycation and lipoxidation end products—amplifiers of inflammation: The role of food." *Journal of Parental Enteral Nutrition* 31, no. 5 (Sep–Oct 2007): 430–40.

Collett, C., B. Evans, G. Hayden, and D. Pappas. "Parental knowledge about common respiratory infections and antibiotic therapy in children." *Southern Medical Journal* 92.10 (Apr 2009): 971. www.ncbi.nlm.nih.gov/pmc/articles/PMC1113842/.

Cordain, Loren. *The Paleo Diet*. Hoboken, NJ: John Wiley & Sons, 2002.

———. "Cereal grains: Humanity's double-edged sword." *World Review of Nutrition and Dietetics* 84 (1999): 19–73.

Cordain, L., L. Toohey, M. J. Smith, and M. S. Hickey. "Modulation of immune function of dietary lectins in rheumatoid arthritis." *British Journal of Nutrition* 83 (2000): 207–17.

Davis, William. *Wheat Belly*. New York: Rodale, 2011.

Dohan, F. C. "Wartime changes in hospital administration for schizophrenia: A comparison of admissions for schizophrenia and other psychoses in six countries during World War II." *Acta Psychiatrica Scandinavic* 42, no. 1 (1966): 1–23.

Drago, S., R. El Asmar, M. Di Pierro, M. Grazia Clemente, et al. "Gliadin, zonulin and gut permeability: Effects on celiac and non-celiac intestinal mucosa and intestinal cell lines." *Scandinavian Journal of Gastroenterology* 41, no. 4 (Apr 2006): 408–19.

D'Souza, A., C. Rajkumer, J. Cooke, and C. Bulpitt. "Probiotics in prevention of antibiotic associated diarrhoea: meta-analysis." *BMJ* 324 (2002): 1361. www.bmj.com/content/324/7350/1361.short.

Giuliano, M., M. Barza, N. Jacobus, and S. Gorbach. "Effect of broad-spectrum parenteral antibiotics on composition of intestinal microflora of humans." *Antimicrobial Agents and Chemotherapy* 31, no. 2 (Feb 1987): 202–206. http://aac.asm.org/content/31/2/202.short.

Guttman, J. A., and B. B. Finlay. "Tight junctions as targets of infectious agents." *Biochimica Biophyicas Acta (BBA) Biomembranes* 1788, no. 4 (Apr 2009): 832–41.

Hadjivassiliou, M., S. Sanders, R. Grünewald, N. Woodroofe, et al. "Gluten sensitivity: From gut to brain." *Lancet* 9, no. 3 (Mar 2010): 318–30.

Jernberg, C., S. Löfmark, C. Edlund, and J. Jansson. "Long-term ecological impacts of antibiotic administration on the human intestinal microbita." *The ISME Journal* 1, no. 1 (2007): 56. http://www.nature.com/ismej/journal/v1/n1/abs/ismej20073a.html.

Jernberg, C., S. Löfmark, and C. Edlund. "Long-term impacts of antibiotic exposure on the human intestinal microbiota." *Microbiology* 156, no. 11 (2010): 3216–3223. http://mic.sgmjournals.org/content/156/11/3216.full.pdf+html.

Kraft, B., and E. Westman. "Schizophrenia, gluten, and low-carbohydrate, ketogenic diets: A case report and review of the literature." *Nutrition & Metabolism* 26, no. 6 (Feb 2009): 10.

Krasowska, A., A. Dyjankiewicz, M. Lykaszewicz, and D. Dziadkowiec. "The antagonistic effect of Saccharomyces boulardii on Candida albicans filamentation, adhesion and biofilm formation." *FEMS Yeast Research* 9, no. 8 (2009): 1312–1321. http://onlinelibrary.wiley.com/doi/10.1111/j.1567-1364.2009.00559.x/full.

McFarland, L., C. Surawicz, R. Greenberg, R. Fekety, et al. "A randomized placebo-controlled trial of Saccharomyces boulardii in combination with standard antibiotics for Clostridium difficile disease." *Journal of the American Medical Association* 271, no. 24 (1994): 1913–1918. www.biocodex.com.tr/wp-content/uploads/antibiyotik03.pdf.

Niederhofer, H., and K. Pittschieler, K. "A preliminary investigation of ADHD symptoms in persons with celiac disease." *Journal of Attention Disorder* 10, no. 2 (Nov 2006): 200–204.

Pynnönen, P., E. Isometsä, M. Verkasalo, S. Kähkönen, et al. "Gluten-free diet may alleviate depressive and behavioural symptoms in adolescents with coeliac disease: A prospective follow-up case-series study." *BMC Psychiatry* 17, no. 5 (Mar 2005): 14.

Roizen, Michael, and Mehmet D. Oz. *You on a Diet: The Owner's Manual for Waist Management.* New York: Free Press, 2006.

Selinger, C. P., A. Bell, A. Cairns, M. Lockett, et al. "Probiotic VSL#3 prevents antibiotic-associated diarrhoea in a double-blind, randomized, placebo-controlled clinical trial." *Journal of Hospital Infection* 84, no. 2 (2013): 159–165. www.sciencedirect.com/science/article/pii/S0195670113001102.

Shira Idit, D., P. Hibberd, and S. Gorbach. "Probiotics for prevention of antibiotic-associated diarrhea." *Journal of Clinical Gastroenterology* 42 (2008): S58–S63. http://journals.lww.com/jcge/Abstract/2008/07001/Probiotics_for_Prevention_of_Antibiotic_associated.4.aspx.

Tatham, A. S., and P. R. Shewry. "Allergens to wheat and related cereals." *Clinical & Experimental Allergy* 38, no. 11 (Nov 2008): 1712–26.

Verdu, E. F., D. Armstrong, and J. A. Murray. "Between celiac disease and irritable bowel syndrome: The 'no man's land' of gluten sensitivity." *American Journal of Gastroenterology* 104, no. 6 (Jun 2009): 1587–94.

Wolf, Robb. *The Paleo Solution: The Original Human Diet.* Las Vegas, NV: Victory Belt Publishing, 2010.

# CHAPTER 5:
## Activity: Moving and Fueling for Maximized Benefit

Ballantyne, Coco. "Does exercise really make you healthier?" *Scientific American*, Jan 2009, 26.

Taubes, Gary. "Does exercise really make us thinner?" *New York Magazine*, Oct 1, 2007.

————. "The scientist and the stairmaster: Why most of us believe exercise makes us thinner and most of us are wrong." *New York Magazine*, Sep 24, 2007.

# PART III: YOUR BODY, YOUR RULES

## CHAPTER 6:
## A Step-by-Step Guide to Self-Monitoring

Adiels, M., S. Olofsson, M. Taskinen, and J. Borén. "Overproduction of very low-density lipoproteins is the hallmark of the dyslipidemia in the metabolic syndrome." *Arteriosclerosis, Thrombosis and Vascular Biology* 28, no. 7 (Jul 2008): 1225–36.

Brainerd, H., S. Margen, and M. J. Chatton. *Current Diagnosis and Treatment.* Los Altos, CA: Lange Medical Publications, 1962.

Breneman, James C. *Basics of Food Allergy.* Springfield, IL: Charles C. Thomas, 1984.

Cordain, L. "Implications for the role of diet in acne." *Seminars in Cutaneous Medicine and Surgery* 24, no. 2 (Jun 2005): 84–91.

Davis, William. *Wheat Belly.* New York: Rodale, 2011.

Hadaegh, F., D. Khalili, A. Ghasemi, M. Tohidi, et al. "Triglyceride/HDL-cholesterol ratio is an independent predictor for coronary heart disease in a population of Iranian men." *Nutrition Metabolism and Cardiovascular Disease* 19, no. 6 (Jul 2009): 401–8.

Kock, Ned. "Large LDL and small HDL particles: The best combination." *Health Correlator* (blog), Feb 16, 2010. http://healthcorrelator.blogspot.com/2010/02/large-ldl-and-small-hdl-particles-best.html.

Kresser, Chris. "How to prevent diabetes and heart disease for 16 dollars." *Chris Kresser L.Ac: Medicine for the 21st Century* (blog), Nov 26, 2011. http://chriskresser.com/how-to-prevent-diabetes-and-heart-disease-for-16.

————. "Why hemoglobin A1c is not a reliable marker." *Chris Kresser L.Ac: Medicine for the 21st Century* (blog), Mar 11, 2011. http://chriskresser.com/why-hemoglobin-a1c-is-not-a-reliable-marker.

————. "5 reasons not to worry about your cholesterol numbers." *Chris Kresser L.Ac: Medicine for the 21st Century* (blog), Jan 26, 2011. http://chriskresser.com/5-reasons-not-to-worry-about-your-cholesterol-numbers.

Lamarche, B., I. Lemieux, and J. P. Després. "The small, dense LDL phenotype and the risk of coronary heart disease: Epidemiology, pathophysiology and therapeutic aspects." *Diabetes & Metabolism* 25, no. 3 (Sep 1999): 199–211.

Leckart, Steven. "Blood Simple." *Wired*, Dec 2010.

Lemos da Luz, P., D. Favarato, J. R. Faria-Neto, P. Lemos, et al. "High ratio of triglycerides to HDL-cholesterol predicts extensive coronary disease." *Clinics* 63, no. 4 (Aug 2008): 427–32.

McCraty, R., M. Atkinson, and D. Tomasino. "Impact of a workplace stress reduction program on blood pressure and emotional health in hypertensive employees." *The Journal of Alternative and Complementary Medicine* 9, no. 3 (2003): 355–369.

Otvos, J. D., E. J. Jeyarajah, and W. C. Cromwell. "Measurement issues related to lipoprotein heterogeneity." *American Journal of Cardiology* 90, no. 8A (Oct 17, 2002): 22i–29i.

Packard, C. J. "Triacylglycerol-rich lipoproteins and the generation of small, dense low-density lipoprotein." *Biochemical Society Transactions* 31, no. 5 (Oct 2003): 1066–69.

Ravnskov, Uffe. *Ignore the Awkward: How the Cholesterol Myths Are Kept Alive.* Uffe Ravnskov, 2010.

Ruhl, Jenny. "What is a normal blood sugar?" *Blood Sugar 101.* http://bloodsugar101.com.

Saxena, P., A. Prakash, and A. Nigam. "Efficiency of 2-hour post glucose insulin levels in predicting insulin resistance in polycystic ovarian syndrome with infertility." *Journal of Human Reproductive Sciences* 4, no. 1 (Jan 2011): 20–22.

Sisson, Mark. "How to interpret cholesterol test results." *Mark's Daily Apple* (blog), Dec 21, 2011. www.marksdailyapple.com/how-to-interpret-cholesterol-test-results.

Smith, R. N, N. J. Mann, A. Braue, H. Mäkeläinen, et al. "A low-glycemic-load diet improves symptoms in acne vulgaris patients: A randomized controlled trial." *American Journal of Clinical Nutrition* 86, no. 1 (Jul 2007): 107–15.

Sniderman, A. D. "How, when, and why to use apolipoprotein B in clinical practice." *American Journal of Cardiology* 90, no. 8A (Oct 17, 2002): 48i–54i.

Thom, Dick. *Coping with Food Intolerances,* 4th ed. New York: Sterling, 2002.

Younis, N., R. Sharma, H. Soran, V. Charlton-Menys, et al. "Glycation as an atherogenic modification of LDL." *Current Opinion in Lipidology* 19, no. 4 (Aug 2008): 378–84.

# ABOUT THE AUTHOR

Ashley Tudor is a design strategist who has worked with Fortune 500 companies and small start-ups to tackle tough health-related issues. Her work has included creating dieting programs, designing strategies to help food companies fight obesity, conceiving new medical devices for primary care physicians, and developing online tools to help people use food as medicine. In recognition of her work, Ashley was named one of San Francisco's Top Innovators in Health in 2010.

Ashley advocates a Paleo or "real food" diet from quality sources. She is an avid outdoorsman, hunter, and field-to-table chef. She loves any excuse to get into the mountains, valleys, and fields, especially to search out her own food. She has won a national award for her easy, healthy, delicious recipes.

Ashley seeks to apply new technologies to give people tools to take control of their own health, avoid disease altogether, and work effectively with health-care providers. She focuses on moving the dialogue beyond "calories in, calories out" and providing frameworks to help people engage with their health. She is an avid self-tracker and a member of the Quantified Self community.

Ashley is the author of *Sweet Potato Power: Smart Carbs, Paleo and Personalized.* She has been a visiting lecturer at Stanford University, the Wharton School of the University of Pennsylvania, and IDSA. She studied political economy and sociology at Dartmouth College and Oxford University. Ashley lives and works in San Francisco.

# INDEX